CONFESSIONS
OF A
FUNERAL
DIRECTOR

CONFESSIONS OF A
FUNERAL
DIRECTOR

HOW THE
BUSINESS
OF DEATH
SAVED
MY LIFE

CALEB WILDE

HarperOne
An Imprint of HarperCollinsPublishers

CONFESSIONS OF A FUNERAL DIRECTOR. Copyright © 2017 by Caleb Wilde. All rights reserved. Printed in the United States of America. No part of this book may be used or reproduced in any manner whatsoever without written permission except in the case of brief quotations embodied in critical articles and reviews. For information, address HarperCollins Publishers, 195 Broadway, New York, NY 10007.

HarperCollins books may be purchased for educational, business, or sales promotional use. For information, please e-mail the Special Markets Department at SPsales@harpercollins.com.

FIRST EDITION

Designed by Yvonne Chan
Artwork by Rvector/Shutterstock
Photograph on page ix by Nicole Wilde

Library of Congress Cataloging-in-Publication Data has been applied for.

ISBN 978-0-06-246524-5

17 18 19 20 21 LSC 10 9 8 7 6 5 4 3 2 1

CONTENTS

AUTHOR'S NOTE

As a funeral director in Parkesburg, Pennsylvania, I've been privy to some very personal moments. I've been told private stories in trust and confidence. I've seen terrible things that are better left untold. I've witnessed people's most vulnerable moments. As an effort not to betray my community's trust, many of the following stories have been Frankensteined. They contain fragments of stories that I've pieced together to create something unique that maintains both the integrity of my own journey and the privacy of others' journeys. Some names have also been changed to protect the privacy of these individuals and families.

The author, Caleb Wilde *(right),* with his father *(left),* and grandfather *(center).*

1

DEATH NEGATIVE

It was nearly six in the morning when I heard the sounds of hovering helicopters a couple hundred yards away from my house. At the time, my wife, Nicki, and I lived in a small half of a double on the farthest fringe of the Borough of Parkesburg. While the occasional helicopter could be heard in Parkesburg proper, our little house on Upper Valley Road was sandwiched by the sounds of the trains that ran on the tracks a hundred feet from our small backyard and the speeding cars on Upper Valley a mere twenty feet from our front door.

I peeked my head outside the window but couldn't see the machines that were producing the sounds I could so clearly hear. The idea that something must be very wrong entered my mind. I turned on the television, and sure enough, the Philadelphia station I turned on had a Breaking News update. The rhythmed and practiced voice of the news anchor read the prompter with all the outward concern he could exercise: "Two young boys and their aunt and uncle died in a fiery car crash outside of Parkesburg, Chester County, late last night."

Parkesburg is an hour outside of Philadelphia. We're the small town of thirty-five hundred that claims Philadelphia as our closest "big city" while Philadelphia has no idea we even exist, except when something horrific happens. This morning, Parkesburg had made the news. Today, Philadelphia reporters descended upon Parkesburg to fill their 6 A.M. quota.

There have been a few times when Facebook has informed me of a death before the family has called us at the Wilde Funeral Home. But this was the first time I had turned on the television and watched aerial footage of a disaster that was soon to be passed on to me. When I got to the funeral home later that morning, I learned we were the ones entrusted to handle the services for all four of the deceased. The two adults (the aunt and uncle of the boys, who were babysitting the boys at that time) were to be cremated, while the boys, eight and ten years of age, were to be embalmed and viewed, depending on the condition of their bodies.

The following day—after the coroner performed her duty—I drove our van to remove the two adults first (our removal van comfortably fits two in the supine position). After I dropped them off at the funeral home, I jumped back in the van to pick up the bodies of the two boys. When I go on these tragic calls, I'll usually either sit in silence or find some upbeat music on the radio to distract me from the void. It can be anything: Pop music. Oldies. Katy Perry.

After driving the bodies home, it was my duty to unzip the body bags for the two boys to see if their faces could be made presentable for a public viewing. The smell of burnt human flesh is somewhat distinct. It's not like the smell of barbecuing chicken or a pig on the spit. It sticks to your hair, to your clothing, and when I opened those bags, what I saw will forever stick in my mind. You've seen the Hollywood versions of burn victims, and it's all horrible, but the visuals we see on the TV screen don't do justice to these tragic deaths. Tragic deaths have a presence about them, something that can't be captured by the makeup and advanced special effects. All deaths have a type of presence, but tragic deaths have a presence that fills a room. I don't know if I believe in ghosts, but I do believe that the dead have some kind of aura.

I had to look at the boys' faces to determine whether or not we could have a viewing, hoping to find a visage that could—through hours of work—be presentable to the family. Unfortunately, I didn't find what I was looking for and had to inform their stricken parents that a public viewing was outside of our ability, which—in a way—produces a small sense of guilt in me. Whether the pressure is from an inward or an outward expectation, there's always this nagging feeling that we should be able to restore any form of disfigurement, that embalmers should possess some Harry Potter magic in our prep room and magically wave our trocar (a large needle-like instrument we use during embalming) while chanting *Abracadabra, pulchra cadaver* and then "poof"—we have beautiful corpses. But there is no magic trocar. And there are no mystical chants.

The family was broken in more ways than one. They were fighting about who would officiate the service. One part of the family wanted a nonreligious service while the other side wanted a Christian service. Threats were made. Words were spoken that should never be spoken, and we had to involve the police. The day before the service a police officer came to the funeral home to go over the plan of action if the funeral became volatile.

As we were going over the funeral procession route with the officer, I collapsed and momentarily lost consciousness; the policeman called the ambulance, and I was taken to the hospital's emergency room with what would later be generically diagnosed as physical exhaustion.

On my way to the hospital, not knowing what was happening to me, I had a moment of unshackled clarity: *Did I want to continue working in this profession? Was this what I wanted to do? Is this who I wanted to be?*

MONTHS BEFORE I FOUND myself in the back of that ambulance, watching the strobe lights bounce off nearby houses and road signs, I found myself struggling with depression and compassion fatigue. My doctor had prescribed me antidepressants to combat the day-to-day experience of depression, but there wasn't anything rejuvenating my burnout. Life lost its value. I lost empathy. And the boundaries that stood between me and self-harm became fragile.

The first couple years of working at the funeral home, I felt like a duck swimming in deep water. From the outside, I was calm, confident, and natural, but underneath, I was kicking furiously against the darkness. Although I knew what I was getting into when I joined the funeral business, it wasn't my closeness to death that was destroying me, it was how I viewed it. I saw death as a certain kind of darkness that needed religion and some degree of flat-out denial to make it ever so slightly lighter and brighter. I assumed that there's nothing good in death. If someone had suggested to me then that there's beauty in death, that there's goodness in death, that death could inspire a healthy spirituality, I would have thought them both morose and naive.

Even though I had grown up around death, I was just as susceptible as anyone to what I call the "death negative narrative" that so many of us have come to believe. On a practical level, I had seen too many tragic, traumatic, and horrific deaths portrayed on TV, on the Internet, and at work. These extremes had normalized the bad deaths so that I had come to think *all* deaths were bad. It's not entirely my fault that I had bought into the death negative narrative. Tragic death sells news. It's great clickbait. It keeps the cycle rolling. But in normalizing the extremes, my perspective about death had been painted in black and it only heightened my mortality fears and strengthened the monster.

Besides the normalization of extremes via the media, the death negative narrative is wired into our very biology. Humans are a most advanced death-defying machine. We have highly evolved systems to fight against the onslaught of death, foremost of which is a brain that sets us above all our competition. And that brain has kept us alive and given us the chance to evolve through its fight-or-flight mechanisms. Death is our oldest evolutionary enemy, and we are so advanced at fighting it that for about fifty to ninety years, most of us win. Still, fearing death is part of our biology; it numbs our minds whenever we try to think about it, and even the most rational among us struggles to find clarity when confronted with the death negative narrative.

Another thing that made me susceptible to the death negative narrative is that even though I had seen thousands of dead bodies, I had never seen someone die. Many have had the privilege of holding the hand of a loved one as he or she passed, but many others of us haven't, in part because the dying process has been isolated in nursing homes and hospitals. In times past and in many other cultures outside the United States, death and dying happen in the home and community, with family and friends acting as death doulas, leading the dying through their final life stage. Today, though, doctors and nurses have replaced family and friends, an unintended consequence of the advancement of medical science. We fear death because we don't know it, we don't see it, and we don't touch it. And what we don't know, we've painted in broad strokes of darkness and negativity. The death negative narrative wouldn't be so strong if we only had the ability to see, touch, and hold our dying and our dead.

My Christian upbringing also contributed to my negative perspective about death. Many Christians teach that death is the punishment—a curse—for the horrible act of sin. All of us are stained with mortality; it's not a natural part of who we are, nor is it something that's healthy for our species. Death is to be fought in every case, just like our sin. The idea that can come out of this is that we are meant for something more than death and as long as we are mortal, we will never be enough.

I needed a new view of death. So I had to tell myself a new story. Death is dark, but it's also light, and between that contrast I saw a death positive narrative begin to appear.[1] The dark and light can produce a rainbow of color that exists in a spectrum of hues, shades, tints, and values. Its beauty is firmly planted in the storm, but we've become color-blind. And I tremble to say there's good in death, that there's a death positive narrative, because I've looked in the eyes of the grieving mother and I've seen the heartbreak of the stricken widow, but I've also seen something more in death, something good. Death's hands aren't all bony and cold.

Some may hear me say *There's a death positive narrative* and think I'm saying *Death isn't as hard as you think it is.* Let me be clear, that's not what I'm saying. Death is as hard, if not harder, than any of us can imagine. I'm saying we've heard an incomplete narrative. Death is like mud; it's dirty, messy, and incredibly tough to walk through, but, surprisingly, it holds vital ingredients to life, and when seeds are planted, it can help sprout new life.

Death isn't just the dirty and the messy. We see death as a loss, and it is. But in death, we often find our most honest self, a stronger community, and some find that they are able to overcome the fear of death and live life to the fullest. It's not a supermodel-type beauty that is genetically ingrained in the DNA of death, but a beauty of struggle and resiliency that, in the end, can produce a spectrum of growth.

FOR MUCH OF MY LIFE, I tried to find meaning outside of death— and outside of death care—because I feared it, and I assumed it was only negative, but as I was riding in the back of the ambulance that day, I was finally desperate enough to look past the death negative narrative and attempt to positively reframe death. If I was to stay in the business of undertaking, this was my last straw. I was depressed, and if I couldn't find something good in death itself, I knew I'd either have to quit or I'd succumb to self-harm or unhealthy self-medication. I wasn't looking to glorify pain or paint suffering as categorically redemptive, but deep inside, my survivor instinct kicked in and unlike my evolutionary ancestors, my survival in death care depended on my ability to lean into death.

I was at rock bottom in the back of the ambulance. For the first time in a long time, strapped down on the gurney, I looked up. We look up, and sometimes we find that the rock-bottom experience is somehow a mountaintop experience, because for the first time in a long time we can see the light at the top.

It occurred to me that I had a choice, that I could leave the funeral business, that I was someone who could choose what I wanted to be. It's invigorating to remember that we have some degree of freedom in life, in our relationships and our vocations. Nobody would have blamed me if I had chosen to leave the funeral home that day. I could have claimed that it was too much for me to handle, left the family business, and tried something else. Instead, the next day, against the doctor's orders, I showed up for work.

Not because I was a Wilde.

Not because it was a way to pay the bills.

Not because it was what the Parkesburg community wanted for me.

Not because I needed to help out my dad and my grandfather.

But because I wanted to do it.

This book is my journey from believing the death negative narrative to finding something more in death. It's the story of reluctantly joining my family's funeral business, having my personal beliefs called into question, and eventually finding the positive side of death and death care. It's a hard story, not something you'd talk about over a plate of spaghetti and meatballs. But, for me, it has become a good journey, where I've found a renewed sense of spirituality formed in the cauldron of mortality.

I wanted to find life in death and find the life of being a funeral director.

2

PLAYTIME IN THE
CASKET ROOM

I was born from a *Romeo and Juliet*–type relationship—if *Romeo and Juliet* had been set in a funeral home. My dad is the fifth generation of Wilde funeral directors, and my mother would have been the fourth generation of Brown funeral directors had she joined the family business.

After my mother grew up watching her dad work the tough hours and stressful environment of the funeral business, she vowed never to be a funeral director herself or to marry into the business. She often tells the story of how her mom, dad, and two sisters would head out on vacation and would stop at a pay phone to call the funeral home to check in. If someone died, they'd walk with pissy looks on their faces back into the car and drive back to the funeral home, end of vacation.

My dad has an even worse vacation story. He, his parents, and his two sisters hopped into the family station wagon to drive eighteen hours from Pennsylvania to Florida to see Mickey Mouse at Disney World. My dad and his sisters were so excited, but as soon as they crossed the Florida line, his dad called to check in at the funeral home and learned that there had been a death and he was needed back to take care of it. Heartbroken, the kids got back into the car to drive eighteen hours straight back to Pennsylvania. Death waits for no one, not even a date with Mickey Mouse.

In life's funny way, despite my mother's firm conviction that she'd never marry a funeral director, she'd end up marrying the son of a competing funeral family from a neighboring town. When she met my dad working stage crew on their high school play, he wasn't the stereotypical morbid son of an undertaker. Unlike some of his fellow students in his funeral school, he didn't consider embalming roadkill an enjoyable pastime. He had long hair that framed his John Lennon glasses and was fun loving.

He also wasn't set on joining the family business upon graduating from high school. Like many who grow up under the pressures of a family business, he initially "rebelled" by following his gifts and dreams. He became an apprentice gunsmith at Colonial Williamsburg and later worked in construction, restoring Colonial homes. By the time I was born, the obligation my dad felt to join the family business had overtaken his creative passions, and he fell into his role as the fifth generation of Wilde funeral directors.

That means that on my dad's side, the Wilde side, I'm a sixth-generation funeral director and on my mom's side, the Brown side, I would have been a fifth-generation funeral director. I like to say I'm a thoroughbred funeral director; my blood runs full with roughly nine generations of undertaking pedigree. As far as I know, I'm the only one of my kind.

Growing up, the domestic and professional areas blended together in our family-run funeral home business. Like most "mom-and-pop" businesses, the family funeral home is being bought out by large corporate funeral homes, but my mother's childhood home was both the Brown Funeral Home and my grandparents' house. It didn't have the feel of a corporate-run funeral home but had smells, decorations, and designs unique to my ma-maw's tastes.

One of my favorite games as a child was to play hide-and-seek with my cousins in the casket room. We'd crawl around the plush carpet on the floor of the showroom, ears listening for the giggles or sounds of one another. It was a risky move for my grandfather Brown, a kindhearted but conservative person, to let his four young grandkids play in this room. Caskets aren't cheap things. Even the "plain pine box" costs about the same as a used moped. We slinked around the various galvanized steel and wood caskets looking for hiding spots, carefully making sure we didn't touch the exteriors lest our little fingerprints tarnish the polished surfaces. We'd hide under them, behind them, but never in them. That was the only rule.

Both sets of grandparents lived at their respective funeral homes. Our family gatherings and regular Sunday visits were held at their homes, so naturally, seeing dead people was a regular occurrence for my cousins and me. The bodies were much more visible to us at the Brown Funeral Home, because Pop-Pop and Ma-Maw Brown had their living space on the funeral home's first floor. Their dining room and living room were multipurpose rooms. By rearranging the chairs, these rooms changed from seating areas for death and grief to rooms for family and holiday celebrations. The same room could be filled with tears one hour and the next it would be filled with the laughter of children and Ma-Maw's delicious food. It sounds strange, and maybe a little scary, to be surrounded by so much death as a kid, but the fact of death was a normal part of my life that initially existed comfortably in my childhood outlook.

The funeral home's chapel was adjacent to the family living room, allowing us to jump literally from a life area to a dead-person area. Even though the boundary between the living room and the chapel was a thin wall, whenever a corpse was set out in the chapel, a hush fell over us as we entered. The chapel felt like an entirely independent area, housing something entirely foreign. We entered the chapel on tiptoes, like we were interrupting something sacred.

On the other side of the family, the Wilde Funeral Home housed the business on the first floor while my grandparents lived on the second floor. In fact, Pop-Pop Wilde was born in one of the bedrooms on the second floor. The bedroom where my grandfather was born is now home to his oft-used early-1980s, faded burgundy La-Z-Boy rocking chair. If all goes according to his plan, he'll die in his rocking chair and so hold the distinction of being a man who both entered this world and left it in the same room.

In both funeral homes, I had been given clear instruction by Pop-Pop Wilde and Pop-Pop Brown that I was never, under any circumstances, to go into the morgue. I was told it was because there were dangerous chemicals and tools, and also that it was technically illegal because I wasn't licensed . . . yet. But a couple of times I snuck a peek at what went on behind the closed morgue door where danger, mystery, and death collided. I remember one instance when I followed Ma-Maw Brown from the kitchen to the morgue; she opened the door to relay a message to Pop-Pop, and I caught a glimpse of my grandfather dressed in a mask, gloves, and full protective garments. The smell that poured out of the room was that of a strong cleaning solution. The lights were industrial bright, and the morgue table was pitched at a slight angle, with the head of the dead man at the top, and the feet below. A single paper towel covered his genitals. All this was set to the ambient noise of fans that were so loud Ma-Maw had to raise her voice for Pop-Pop to hear her. Ma-Maw was all things practical at the funeral home. She worked the funerals, answered the business phone, cooked the family dinners, kept the house in order while Pop-Pop was all business. She was COO to Pop-Pop's CEO.

Standing beside the dead body was Pop-Pop. The morgue table was little more than waist high, allowing him to survey the whole thing. He had a large needle in the dead person's stomach, and he was slowly but authoritatively moving it around. As quickly as I saw it, the door shut. No blood, no guts. No ghosts or strange noises. I had yet to be desensitized by the stylized violence of movies and video games, nor did I completely understand that death meant the deceased could no longer feel the pain of a massive needle stuck in his stomach. I thought that the needle must be hurting the poor dead guy in some way and there was a slight rise of anger toward my grandfather who was moving this thing (which I would later know as a trocar) throughout the dead man's abdomen.

I suppose what made my experience with death slightly different was that death was an object for me, not yet personal. Two of my closest middle school friends lost family members, a father for one, a sister for the other. But I didn't lose my father. I didn't lose my sister to death. For me, death was work. Death care was the family tradition. And I think that's why I wasn't a morbid kid—I didn't play with a Ouija board in the cemetery or enjoy the vivisection of small animals. I looked like any other kid growing up in the '80s. I had my collection of Transformers, my Reebok Pumps and clothing that was picked from the discount racks of JCPenney. My morbid upbringing expressed itself in different ways than a proclivity toward all things dark. But, it did, without a doubt, make me different.

I *was* different. Even though death wasn't personal, the idea of death saturated my youth. And the thought of what might come after death consumed me, and eventually broke me.

3

BROKEN OPEN

As a child, as normal as it was to grow up around caskets and dead bodies, it did make me sensitive to the shortness of life. I never had that carefree, invincible feeling of youth as the cloud of my mortality hung thick over my mind. At night, I'd often lie in bed and instead of thinking about becoming a professional baseball player or dreaming about a red Lamborghini Countach, I'd be thinking about my death, wondering when and how it would take place, and what would happen after it. Death inspired the larger questions:

What does dying feel like?

What happens after I die?

Is death final?

Is there a heaven? Is there a hell?

Why doesn't God help the suffering people?

And, sometimes, although rarely, I'd wonder if maybe I could drive a Countach in heaven since I couldn't afford one on earth.

As a child, death and religion twined together. Death and religion are often intimate partners; you might even say that death is the source of religion. Our fear of death, our heartbreak from it, and our desire for a better world create the cauldron for some—if not most—of our religious pursuits. And not only does one help create the other, but both share similarities. Like religion, death is shrouded in a sense of the sacred, the unspeakable, and the emotive. Like the religious experience, death is better understood through symbols and art and stories. Death and dying are sacred arts of the human condition, where we learn about ourselves, build community, and contemplate meaning, much like houses of religion.

But this relationship between death and religion isn't always healthy. My childhood pursuit of the big questions found its direction in my conservative Protestant family, where we were raised with these types of prayers:

> *Now I lay me down to sleep,*
> *I pray the Lord my soul to keep,*
> *If I shall die before I wake*
> *I pray the Lord my soul to take.*

In other words, if I die tonight in my sleep, God, please don't let my soul burn in hell.

My young mind was apt to fantasy and conjured up worlds that were just as real to me as the actual one in a type of magical thinking, where fantasy and reality intermixed. And it's an art that can be horribly frightening when our gift of imagination is focused on the worst made-up fantasy of them all: hell. To pick up on a popular office supply company slogan, hell is the "easy button" for behavioral control, and it has too often been abused by religion. This behavior control goes something like this: if you don't do what we tell you, you'll be thrown into a lake of fire where your skin will melt into goo like Nazi Gestapo agent Arnold Ernst Toht in the Indiana Jones film *Raiders of the Lost Ark*. But as much as religions use this concept of hell to control their faithful, I'm not sure most people believe their friends and family go there.

A couple of years ago my dad had a bumper sticker on the back end of his rusted-out '86 Ford F-150. It said "Live So the Pastor Doesn't Have to Lie at Your Funeral." There's some truth to that bumper sticker. Of the nearly four thousand funerals I've worked, I have never once heard a pastor state conclusively that the person they are memorializing was a bad person, although I've heard thousands of eulogies that state conclusively that the deceased is in heaven!

Pastors have done some fancy preaching for those who have lived less than generous, kind, and loving lives. I remember one pastor saying about a man who blatantly hated most everyone, especially God, "This man didn't like God, but he was a man who loved the outdoors. And anybody who loves the outdoors is a lover of God because God created the outdoors. Such a lover of the outdoors is enjoying the great outdoors called 'heaven' right now." Honestly, contrary to my dad's cheesy bumper sticker, I don't think pastors are lying. I think pastors have the hope that the deceased finds himself or herself in the presence of God. Hell, for most believers, is only reserved for the likes of Hitler, Joffrey Baratheon, and the Others, but hardly ever for their own.

Just like the preachers, most of us hardly ever believe that our friend, our family member, or our loved one is suffering in the lake of fire. Hell is where people go who aren't like us, or who aren't like what *our* God wants us to be. Hell is the most awful form of othering, a place that is simply too horrible, too awful a torment for us to believe that anyone we know is going there for all eternity. It's so horrible that we can only send an idea of someone, or someone we have no empathy toward, no love for. And yet, despite our inability to send those we love to hell, we inexplicably think that a God who is love, a God who knows everyone, a God who is near to the brokenhearted . . . this God who is intimately acquainted with all of us can just capriciously send billions and billions of people to eternal torment. If we, in our love, have such difficulty believing our people go to hell, how much more difficulty would a God of love have in sending God's children there?

But as a young child who had a firm grasp on mortality, and an immature, distorted view of God, I believed that God was sending most of us to hell, including—and especially—me. Night after night I'd lie in bed and do what I could to convince God that I should be saved from the Toht treatment. My childhood God was a God who was broken apart. It was a graceless God of extreme vengeance, a God who would divvy out an eternity of hellfire for a single act of disrespect, for a single sin. The God that I imagined as a child had no reason to love and listen to me, and so my hell fantasy continued unabated.

I wasn't a rebellious kid per se, but my conscience—and Protestant upbringing—told me that hell was what I deserved. It said that I didn't have to be bad to deserve hell, I just had to be human, and sinful. And like any kid, I had my moments, I suppose, when I was sneaky and too curious. In elementary school, I had my moments of exploiting others in baseball card trading, I stole some money from my dad's wallet once or twice, and I had a pizza shop deliver a pizza to my school desk, a creative misdeed that the principal forced me to atone for by cleaning the toilets for an entire week.

But the damning sin of my childhood happened when I was ten years old, and my buddies and I paged through a pile of faded and musty *Playboys* that we had found abandoned in an old dump. None of us had hit puberty or had any concept about how the birds and bees worked, but we got an anatomy lesson from good ol' Hugh Hefner. The *Playboys* were a novelty, a novelty that was sweetened because we all knew this dump-yard find was our forbidden little secret. Secrets are the doorway for children to develop their sense of self. Secrets are the thing that kids have that their parents don't have, the thing that makes them different, private and separate from someone they've been so dependent upon. This secret, these *Playboys*, both became the source of my independence and fortified my damnation.

Childish curiosity soon gave way to the absolute conviction—based on my religious upbringing and my mortality awareness—that I was a sinner who could die at any minute and subsequently be damned to an eternity in hell. This threat of eternity in hell began to reshape my view of death: instead of seeing death as an objective part of life, death was now the irreversible event that led me directly to the lake of fire. Being a "hell-bound" youngster with a newfound death anxiety shaped my personality through middle school and into high school: thinking about hell, death, and God formed a steel cage, trapping my thoughts and feelings inside and making me increasingly introspective. I remember that I'd almost always sit alone on my forty-five-minute bus ride to and from school. Unlike the other kids who would study for their exams or talk with their friends, I'd press my head against the widow and let my mind wander as I thought and felt the heavy things of the world.

Introspection changed to contemplation at the age of fifteen when I started waking up at 4 A.M. every morning to practice my bibliotherapy with theology and spirituality books, a habit that prompted my parents to start calling me "monk." Instead of processing things inwardly, I started to consult the great dead people of our world and contemplate the wonderful books and ideas they left behind. They guided my fear to faith. As I grew and studied, I gravitated to the idea that God was love, not just love in theory, but that God suffered with us, cried with us, and knew the lessons of death. God's love for us is suffering love. As God experiences our pain, God is moved to give. Nicholas Wolterstorff writes that "the tears of God are the meaning of history," which I take to mean that the suffering love of God is the engine, the motivation of God's life.[1] "God so suffered with the world that God gave God's only begotten son"—God's heart was broken open.

The notion of God's suffering love also led me to realize that at the center of God's kingdom wasn't power, judgment, and a desire to damn people to hell, but a desire to uphold and support the weak, the broken, the vulnerable, and the sinful. God's community was for people like me—people afraid of death, people who feel fear, people who feel ashamed of their own shortcomings. And this view of a good God, this theology of God, inspired me to refocus my life from one of shame and guilt to a life that was outwardly focused, with a mission to understand and inspire life. I too had been broken open.

We will all at one time or another be confronted with death, our mortality, and the deeper questions of life. The question isn't *if* we will be broken by death and dying and mortality, but *how* will these inevitabilities break us? Will we be broken open or will death break us apart?

Death and dying isn't something we can tame. We've tried to tame it through medical advancement, but as much as greater understanding might reduce our fear of it, and medical science staves it off, death and dying is wild. For those who are actively dying, this phase can be an experience of losing control of your physical functions, setting the stage for death to come. When it does, it creates a whole different culture for those left behind, where schedules are always in flux, emotions trump mental function, and love trumps control. Death and dying is that definitive experience in adulthood where we reconnect with what it felt like as a child to need, to want, to find dependency again. It's that experience where we reconnect with the wild, but some adults have become too rigid, too in control for the wild of death.

When hardship comes, some hearts are broken apart, and like pottery or glass, those hearts are difficult to put back together. But other hearts are broken open like a fist that opens itself to receive and give back, or like clay that adapts to pressure.[2] Whereas death's wildness can shatter the well-ordered, rigid life, it can open those who have learned to flow with the waves of life. The broken-open heart, the heart that has been molded by pain and suffering, knows to "be kind, for everyone you meet is fighting a battle you know nothing about."[3]

The broken-open heart has room for others' pain.

It uses its own pain to find love for those we don't like.

The broken-open heart seeks to understand.

It's slow to take offense and quicker to forgive.

The broken-open heart uses grace to build and bind the broken.

It welcomes and includes the Other and the Outcast.

Because it knows the pain, it knows the fight; it knows the wild.

The broken-open heart, in many ways, is the heart of a child, the way to the kingdom.

For me, confronting death—and all the questions that came with it—at a young age was the single most difficult and the single most beneficial influence in my life. We think children should be shielded from the difficulties and the void of death, but for me there was no better time to see. It wasn't easy, especially when hell was mixed into the perspective on death. But, in prostrating me to the ground, death has allowed a view of earth and dirt, giving me a perspective I would have otherwise missed, ignored, and feared but where—surprisingly— I've found the seeds and basic elements of my humanity like empathy, selflessness, grace, and understanding. And as I'd later move into a career working around death, I'd see these elements at play over and over. Because it isn't just once that we're broken by death. It's not a once-and-done experience. It happens all throughout life, and each time it happens, we can learn to pivot toward being broken open and allow empathy, selflessness, grace, and understanding to fill our hearts anew.

4

DEATH SABBATH

When I was twelve years old, my grandmother died. It was sudden and too soon—she was only fifty-nine. It was my first close experience with death at a personal level, not just professional. The day after Mom-Mom Wilde's death, we all gathered in Pop-Pop and Mom-Mom's second-floor living room and met with the pastor who would be doing the service. We were all involved, from the in-laws to the youngest of us grandkids. We all talked to the pastor about the Mom-Mom we knew, and he collected our thoughts into what would later become the eulogy. The pastor prayed for us. My youngest cousin farted during the prayer. We all laughed. Never has there been a more needed fart.

Mom-Mom was embalmed by my late great-uncle Jim and his son Jimmy. Neither Dad nor Pop-Pop could bring himself to perform the embalming, although many embalmers do choose to embalm their loved ones. From the outside looking in, embalming a loved one might seem as twisted as the plots on daytime television. To cut skin and raise the carotid artery, fan the organs with a trocar, and drain the liquids of a body that hugged and kissed you seems like a contradiction of love, like a physical violation. As much as embalmers respect the body, a distinct presence has left it, making it seem like something very different than a person. I suppose viewing the body as less than a person is part of how we do what we do. For many embalmers, it's an act of giving, for others an act of coping, and for still others a promise kept.

We allowed the days following Mom-Mom's death to be a Sabbath, a break from the tyranny of the urgent and a time to focus on each other,

our loss,

our tears,

our pain,

our needs,

our tiredness,

our silence,

our laughter,

our love.

I've since learned how Judaism sees the practice of a death Sabbath as a necessity—not a luxury—of healthy self-care. The initial mourning period is called *aninut,* translated as "burial." In this mourning period, mourners are nearing death themselves. It's as though the death of their loved one has sucked the life out of the living. That lives are so sewn together—as individual as we try to make them—that when we lose another, we lose a part of ourselves. Lauren Winner writes that as the mourners border death, they "are exempt from other commandments . . . because only the living are obligated by God's law."[1]

In this tradition, after the burial, the second phase is *shiva,* the first week after burial. During shiva, there's no sex, music, or even shoes, as the mourners don't leave the house. The mourners don't go back to work or school; they stay in the silence and tears of death. When the week of shiva passes, mourners enter the thirty-day-long period called *shloshim,* allowing them the ability to work their way back into the normal life cycles of jobs and music and sex.

My family wasn't Jewish, but in slowing down and observing our own death Sabbath, I like to think that we honored Mom-Mom, and let her death be as good as the life she lived. I learned what a positive and healthy practice this can be surrounding an otherwise difficult time.

When Pop-Pop Brown died at seventy-eight, I was in a much different position. I was an adult and working as a licensed funeral director. By the time he was diagnosed with pancreatic cancer, he was already dying. Impending death doesn't come as a surprise to funeral directors who watch the end play out over and over again. Death is like that friend who gives all the spoilers away to unsolicited listeners. We know the endings of all the stories, including our own. But just because we know the ending, it doesn't mean we know the story or even the final chapter of that story. For all of us—unlike in the movies—it's not the ending that defines us, but how we live out our narrative.

Pop-Pop Brown had a relatively good death. Unlike Mom-Mom Wilde, who died suddenly, he was able to say good-byes and talk to his daughters about how he wanted them to care for their mom; under the care of hospice, he died relatively pain free on April sixth. He got his house in order. But, much unlike my experience with the death of Mom-Mom Wilde, I didn't take time for a death Sabbath. I was the funeral director from start to finish and had little time to be his grandson.

The day I got the call about my grandfather, I was with my other grandfather, Pop-Pop Wilde, who was sitting in his La-Z-Boy recliner with the cordless phone tucked between his thigh and the chair arm. I was sitting in the chair across the room drinking Dunkin' Donuts iced coffee while Pop-Pop gummed down his powdered sugar donut and small hot coffee. At least once a week, Pop-Pop and I find enough of a break in the happenstance of death to share in the communion of the oft burnt Dunkin' Donuts coffee while we chat about times past and times present. Unlike his contemporaries, he rarely tells me the same story twice.

Today, he was telling me about the visit he had just had with Pop-Pop Brown, his former competitor and the father to his daughter-in-law. At the time of the visit, Pop-Pop Brown was nonverbal and under high doses of morphine that rendered him nearly nonresponsive. Pop-Pop Wilde recounted, "I told him, 'If we had joined funeral homes, it would have been Wilde-Brown Funeral Home.' And he squeezed my damn hand as hard as he could," he said with a chuckle.

The phone rang a couple of minutes after the story, and he smacked enough of the powdered donut off his tongue to answer it. It was hospice, informing us my grandfather had died and that my ma-maw, mom, and aunts were waiting for me. The call switched me into work mode. I didn't cry. I didn't have a moment.

My dad should come with me, I thought. I phoned him and let him know. Dad had gone home early to catch up on some maintenance of his nearly three-hundred-year-old Colonial homestead. It's a constant process of painting and repainting, of repairing and updating, but it provides an excellent excuse for him to cut out of the funeral home when he needs some time off from the psychological struggle of working with bereaved persons. Now, though, those bereaved persons were his. His wife. His mother-in-law. His sisters-in-law. And I knew that his role as comforter took precedent over his role as funeral director. The job of being a stable mind was placed upon me.

We loaded the removal van and readied ourselves for the

half-hour trip from Parkesburg to Lancaster. Going on a removal call creates the same feeling you get before you take a test. You've prepared for the test, you know the material, but there's always a surprise waiting for you that could throw your prep out the window. There's an ominous tension that hovers overhead, making small talk and conversation a difficult task. We turn on the radio or sit in silence until we approach our destination, then we talk some logistics. Once the deed is done and we're on our way home, it's the same type of posttest relief that manifests itself in chattiness and lightheartedness. But this trip was entirely different. I knew the family that awaited me, and they all had seen enough of the funeral business to know what I was going to do.

We arrived, and my aunt took me aside and asked, "Can you do this?" My grandfather Brown was a little heavy and I thought she was asking if I was physically strong enough to lift him.

"Oh, sure. I can lift him, no problem."

"No, I know you can lift him, but can you do this?"

She wasn't talking to Caleb Wilde, the funeral director. She was talking to Caleb Wilde, the grandson. It took me a minute to switch from funeral director to grandson, but I gathered myself and said, "Yes." I don't think my answer satisfied her, and I don't think it satisfied me, either.

Pop-Pop and Ma-Maw Brown had a relationship that most of us can only hope to have. Pop-Pop had a jovial sense of humor that kept things lively and light while Ma-Maw was a clock of consistency who kept the family running in the often-tumultuous schedule of the funeral business. Their life together was like a dance; each had a role, and neither would step on the other's toes or throw the other off balance. Pop-Pop provided for Ma-Maw in love, laughter, and material, and Ma-Maw would reciprocate with love, support, and food. She could cook, and he could eat. A fantastic combination that easily placed his weight north of obesity and his body south of healthy. But when Dad and I placed him on the embalming table, it required little effort. The cancer had taken away those extra pounds that made him look like Pop-Pop Brown. Obese bodies are difficult to embalm as the fat often makes the arteries and veins much more difficult to find, raise up, and drain, but Dad and I had little trouble embalming Pop-Pop.

My memories of his funeral are obscure, like most funerals I work. There were two funerals that day, so Dad, Pop-Pop Wilde, and I were at Pop-Pop Brown's church funeral while my uncle Jim and Jimmy were working the other funeral back at the funeral home. Dad didn't work the funeral because he was with my mom, so it was up to Pop-Pop Wilde and I to keep things running smoothly. I lined up the cars for the procession line and then I worked the registrar book, helping people sign in and get a memorial folder. Something like muscle memory clicks in when I work funerals. I can float through a funeral without much thought or contemplation. But I didn't want that day to be muscle memory; I didn't want that funeral to be muscle memory. I vividly remember thinking to myself throughout the process, *I wish I wasn't working this funeral. I wish I was with my family.*

There are two different words that the ancient Greek language used to describe the idea of time. One is *chronos,* which is the linear time we measure with a clock. The other is *kairos,* which has less to do with the measurement and quantity of time and more to do with the *quality* of time. Modern cultures tend to focus on *chronos,* but some cultures still understand the value of *kairos.* America, with all of our focus on *chronos,* has lost track of *kairos.* We rarely inhabit the moment we're in because we're focused on the *next* moment, the next thing we have to do. I know for me, I'm always looking at the next step and I forget the big picture. I forget the deep breath, the contemplation, the laughter of friends, the smell of the lilac bush in spring. At my grandfather's funeral, I missed the moment because I was the funeral director. I missed the pause, the Sabbath, the *kairos* that death gives us.

A couple weeks later I found myself driving through Creek Road, a small road that mimics every twist and turn of Octoraro Creek. It was the very same road that Pop-Pop and Ma-Maw Brown would drive me through as an infant when they were attempting to put me to sleep. Ma-Maw told me a few times that I'd always nod off and promptly wake up as soon as we pulled back into the funeral home. It was night, and I knew the road well enough to keep my car planted on the road. I was thinking about Pop-Pop, and suddenly the tears started flowing. I pulled the car over alongside the road and wept. I had not only lost my grandfather, but I felt like I had lost a piece of my humanity.

WE ALL GRIEVE DIFFERENTLY, and even funeral directors respond in different ways. Some funeral directors cope by taking charge of their loved ones' funerals. Others, like me, suffer in our grief when we attempt to take the yoke of "strong one" for the sake of the family. Grief is as unique as one's relationship with the deceased. No grief is the same. Some forms of grief are healthier than others, but one form of grief isn't right, and neither is someone else's wrong.

Nevertheless, death asks us to pause. It doesn't tell us what we need to do when we pause (there may be nothing to do at all), but it asks us to be in its presence. To sit with it. Listen to it. To lay aside *chronos* and embrace *kairos*. That's what finally caught up with me when I sat weeping in my car, remembering my grandfather, and thinking about how much I would miss him. It's not a moment of weakness but of strength, and we need to be reminded to allow for these natural pauses in life. We will find that death sits at the heart of what it means to be human, and we may just find ourselves when we practice the death Sabbath.

5

SEARCHING FOR THE
DIVINE IN THE DARK

My own death negative narrative was solidified by two experiences—I'll discuss one here and the other in the next chapter—that began a domino effect on my teenage and post–high school life. The first happened during high school—when I first started working at the funeral home during the summer to make some extra change to pay for my book habit.

I was called to the hospital, and when I was told there was no need for the pomp of a hearse or a pickup wagon, I used my 1986 Pontiac 6000 station wagon. It was the first time I used what we call the brown box. The brown box looks like an inconspicuous toolbox, with a couple dings and dents from over fifty years and a couple generations of use, one and a half feet wide by two and a half long, wood, velvet lined. No one knows what I'm doing when I carry the box into the hospital. Nobody is supposed to know. Nobody wants to know. The sad truth is that the brown box is what we use to pick up infants who have died.

On my way back from the hospital I thought about that little brown box. I thought about how it contained all the greatest hopes and fears of humanity in that tiny baby. I thought how it contained the heights of humanity's passions, the height of our joys, the hope of our future, and the very miracle of God. At the same time, this brown box contained the impetus to the deepest questions our minds can ask, the hardest tears we can cry, and the profoundest pain we can feel. All in this little box.

I took the little infant out of the infant-size carrier and placed it on our morgue table. This was the first infant I had picked up from the hospital. The china doll cold porcelain skin lying on top of our old porcelain-veneered morgue table set in a room with the sterile smell of embalming fluid and Clorox-cleaned laminate flooring is still scarred in my memory. I wasn't prepared for the sight. I suppose you can never prepare yourself to see a dead infant, and maybe that's why it made such a lasting impression on my life.

Most infants we bury usually die from some form of birth defect, but this little one died from choking on a plastic mint wrapper. The infant's parents had a Christmas party the night before and someone must have gobbled down a mint to cover up the smell of shrimp or deviled eggs and accidentally dropped the wrapper on the floor. The next morning the parents were occupied with cleaning the house, while their little one somehow grabbed the wrapper and that was it. It was a tragic Christmas for that family.

Stories like this become real-life fables for the children of funeral directors. When I was younger, my grandfather Brown had numerous scare-the-shit-out-of-you stories that he used whenever a favorable time presented itself.

"Caleb, don't lean back on your chair. I buried a kid your age who fell back and broke his neck."

"Yes, Pop-Pop," I said as I steadied my chair, firmly planting all four legs in front of the little kitchen TV.

Another time while we were getting into his big silver Lincoln Continental, he said, "Make sure the headrest is equal to the height of your head. It will really save your neck in a car wreck, unlike poor old Gerald Henderson."

And I can't count the number of times he told me, "When we get autopsied bodies, you can always tell the smokers by their blackened lungs. So don't smoke or you too will turn your lungs black." Both my grandfathers were former cigar smokers who were able to kick the habit so they felt they had the authority to moralize to their grandson about the horrors of "cancer sticks." Now, as one who has embalmed numerous autopsied bodies, including smokers, I've yet to see this "blackened lung," which makes me think they were just trying to scare me straight.

The children of undertakers likely hear such tragic stories of death all throughout their childhood, which may explain why so many of us are risk adverse and anxiety ridden. Maybe the reason funeral home family businesses continue on generation after generation—unlike so many other family businesses—is because their children are afraid to step out into the wild world for fear they'll suffer an untimely, tragic, and horrific demise. Best just to stay close to death than go out into the world and be surprised by it.

These traumatic deaths are also the reason why so many of us funeral directors can have a death negative narrative, even though we see so much good death. It's hard to see the good and normal deaths when these traumatic deaths scream so loudly in our heads, redefining how we view death and re-defining how we view ourselves, how we view the world, and how we view God.

Back to the infant on the table . . . since God played a large role in my life, I couldn't help but wonder how this in-credibly good and loving God could allow such a thing to happen. It seemed God's love wasn't strong enough to rescue this infant's life. Had I been near the infant, I would have picked up the wrapper without question or pulled it out of the infant's mouth. But God, with all God-power and all God-presence and all God-love, did nothing. I pondered whether perhaps God didn't exist, an unsettling thought I entertained on numerous occasions. But that wasn't nearly as unsettling as believing that God did exist and either didn't care or was downright evil.

As we grow and mature in life, both as people navigating this complicated and sometimes difficult world, and as people of faith, we have to come to terms with the problem of evil, and how to best make sense of it all. If God was to maintain a space in my life, I had to reimagine God to be different from this God who had the power to stop tragedy but chose not to do it.

One of the more popular paths to remake God is through the redefinition of God's power, and I found this the most appealing explanation. The redefinition goes like this: In order to keep believing that God is love, we limit God's power by saying that God voluntarily limited God's power when creating humans; that way we absolve God of all the evil by saying that in fact, it's not God who causes it nor can God forcibly stop it. God has chosen to limit God's power by creating you and me, creatures who have the ability to actually oppose God's will and create our own little worlds where God's purpose of love is *not* being accomplished. Evil and misery were never intended. The world isn't the way God intended it to be. Even the popular Lord's Prayer asks for God's kingdom to come here on earth, as it is in heaven, meaning that it's *not* all God's will. That accidents actually happen, sometimes with deadly results. That the little infant who lay on our morgue table was there by legitimate accident and not by some divine plan, or because "God wanted an angel."

By this thinking, if God is limited, then it is up to us, God's people, to help the world become a better place by helping people embrace life and turn to this loving God. The problem of evil could be solved by my good actions and I could let the love of God solve evil through all my acts of love. I am the creator of the good. I can speak it into existence. And maybe, just maybe, my love and good actions could bring other people to God and I could help make the world a more loving place.

Helping people for the sake of God became my positive coping method, and this positive coping method became ever so slightly complex the more I thought about it. I'd like to say that I simply used good deeds to cope with the confrontation of tragedy, but like a form of PTSD, the tragedy of seeing the things I saw at the funeral home at such a young age began to eat away at goodness, and it eventually ate away my hope for the goodness of this world.

6

SACRED DIRT

The idea started to develop as I was confronted with the problem of evil that it fell to me to work to get people to heaven. Experiences I had at the funeral home—like seeing the unexplainable and heart-wrenching death of a small child—further solidified not only my death negative narrative but built up a heaven-centered orientation because if the world was this sad, this capricious, and this heart-wrenching, the best thing I could do was to save people from this corrupt earth and help them get away from here to heaven. With a heaven-centered orientation, tasks like taking care of dead people seemed too small and unimportant because this life just didn't stack up to the life that was to come.

The rest of my high school summer was spent going on late-night death calls, mowing the lawn, washing the cars, working funerals, and cleaning the morgue. Cleaning the morgue is probably like cleaning a public restroom. There's a bunch of weird stains and splatters that take a long time to work out, and you're pretty sure if you licked any of it, you would die a slow and painful death. None of these tasks were very inspiring for a young kid who wanted to spread the love of God and help people get to heaven.

When I worked funerals, lovely little old ladies would tell me, "I'm so glad you're going into the funeral business. Now I can die happy knowing a Wilde will take care of me." A couple women pulled me in closer and whispered, "Remember to shave my facial hair." I'd smile and let them pinch my abnormally chubby cheeks while I thought to myself, *I don't want to spend my life shaving the facial hair of lovely little elderly ladies from Parkesburg.* But I wanted to do something big, something risky, that involved changing the world by bringing people to heaven and not the shaving of unwanted hairs. This realization led me to a second formative experience. I decided I wanted to become a missionary to far-flung locations, where I could share the love of God with people and ensure they were going to heaven after they died.

To persuade me to come into the family business and not go off to the mission field, my simultaneously frugal and generous Pop-Pop Wilde offered to buy me a car and give me a full ride to funeral school. "There's enough good you can do here," he told me, but it fell on deaf ears. "And besides, I know how much you love cars." It was true. If there was anything that was going to pull me back down to earth, it was a clean, sporty car. I remember driving by a used car dealership and seeing a silver Honda Prelude with a sticker price in huge neon yellow numbers pasted on the windshield that was the exact amount of money my grandfather told me he'd give me. And yet despite the allure of having something nicer than the Pontiac 6000, I stuck to my intentions. Pop-Pop, in a complete act of kindness—as well as many others in the Parkesburg community—still financially backed me when I decided to become a missionary upon graduating from high school in 2000, because being a missionary and helping people go to heaven and escape hell was, in my mind, the best way I could create good.

A couple months of missionary training flew by, and in the early part of 2001, I joined a twelve-person humanitarian group and flew on a couple single-engine prop planes to an isolated area in the Madagascan coast jungle. Although I had joined the Christian missionary group with the hope of "saving souls," I ended up on a team much more focused on humanitarian work, a chance occurrence that likely changed the entire outcome of my life. There were two doctors, a couple nurses, and some grunts like me who were just happy to be a part of what was going to be a makeshift medical clinic for an indigenous coastal tribe.

The mosquitoes were as thick as the air at the end of the rainy season. I was nineteen years old and full of vigor, certainty, and vaccination shots. I was a little disappointed that I wasn't doing any evangelism, but I was certain that I was at least being an extension of God's love. After our plane landed, we all jumped into a muddy army-like four-wheel-drive truck that carried us a couple hours deeper along the coast until the truck could go no farther in the mud and water. The truck drivers let us out and we trekked with supply-loaded backpacks for a couple more hours before finally reaching our destination. My boots kept getting suctioned off my feet in the deep mud, so I took them off and welcomed a few worms that would eventually need to be burned out of their fleshly home. By the time we arrived at our destination, it was dark and the African night was covered in a blanket of stars like nothing I had ever seen in the light-crowded sky back home. There was no electricity, no streetlights, and no close cities to diminish the beauty.

During our two-week stay we treated over one thousand people with our limited medical supplies, but my experience with one man changed my perspective forever. The man was about fifty years old with a swollen stomach and a face glazed with the crippling fog of pain. He wasn't dead yet, but he soon would be as he had no access to any modern health care and no money to buy it. We were the only medical care he'd receive. A bad drinking habit and the subsequent cirrhosis was causing ascites, a buildup of painful fluid pressure around his abdomen. The doctors, set on doing something, thought they could ease the pain by draining some fluid. I volunteered to hold him down as they jammed a large syringe into his abdomen, with the hope that it would relieve both his fluid buildup and his pain. He started kicking when they popped the syringe in, and I put my full weight on his lower body, holding down his legs so the doctors could focus on their task. I knew that this act wouldn't solve any problems. I wasn't saving anyone's soul. I was being present in his pain, not solving it. I was there. That was all I could do for him. That was all we could do.

A couple minutes after the doctors were done with the draining, the cloud of pain started to lift from his face and he looked directly in our eyes and whispered in his native Malagasy tongue, "*Misaotra*"—"thank you." His family who had been surrounding him started touching his face and crying over the fact that for a brief time the pain was beginning to subside and he was able to find some degree of mental clarity.

FOR ME, AT THAT point in my life, the death negative narrative and subsequent heaven-centered orientation had resulted in devaluing the good things of this world. It's easy for us all to fall into. We see heavy tragedies in the news—the violence, the displaced refugees, the homelessness, the poverty, the human casualties of war—which add to our personal tragedies of broken homes, sickness, and the struggle to make ends meet. We latch on to such tragedies; fear clouds our minds and causes many people, like myself, to talk about how "this earth is not my home," by which we mean two things. That all the evil, hate, and injustice isn't representative of the place we want to live. And that heaven is the place we were made to live, while the earth is a temporary residence we must travel through until we cross into our eternal home. It's easy to see this world as just a stepping-stone to heaven. We want the beyond, the over there, and mostly the up there, which is why it's hard to cultivate and tend the garden, because by implication of our heaven-centered orientation, the beyond offers the best promise for a better world while this one has already gone to shit.

But sometimes when we focus on the here and now, we see glimpses of some beautiful things that can only happen here, on earth. It brings a family together for just a moment. It relieves pain for just a moment. It cultivates love for just a moment. And for just that moment, we see a glimpse of the glory of the earth. Heaven may be glorious, but so is the earth, and we miss too much when we focus on one to the exclusion of the other.

I FOUND THAT I had traveled to the far reaches of Africa only to discover that maybe the best way I could be an extension of God's love wasn't by waiting and watching for the life to come. I began to see that I had a fantastic opportunity back in the

United States at the funeral home to do good in *this* world. There was still fear, and uncertainty, but I started to hear the whispers of another narrative, a quiet voice that asks us to be present in the here and now, at this moment, in this place, in the ground I was planted, because maybe heaven is here, hiding somewhere behind the fear-inducing tragedies that cloud our eyes.

Along the way, I learned the Jewish concept of *tikkun olam*, which means "the healing of the world" and is accomplished through presence in the midst of the pain. It can be summarized in the phrase "I'm here with you and I love you" and is accomplished through simple acts of presence. It became a rallying cry for me in my work as a funeral director. Rachel Naomi Remen, in an interview with Krista Tippett, describes it as "a collective task. It involves all people who have ever been born, all people presently alive, all people yet to be born. We are all healers of the world. . . . It's not about healing the world by making a huge difference. It's about the world that touches you."[1] Presence and proximity before performance. As I took that to heart, I started to see small, everyday examples of *tikkun olam* everywhere:

When a mother comforts a child, she's healing the world.

Every time someone listens to another—deeply listens—she's healing the world.

A nurse who bathes the weakened body of an elderly patient is healing the world.

The teacher who invests herself in her students is healing the world.

The plumber who makes the inner workings of a house run smoothly is healing the world.

A funeral director who finds that he can heal the world even at his family's business.

When we practice presence and proximity, we may not change anyone, we may not shift culture or move mountains, but it's a healing act, if for none other than ourselves. When we do our work with kindness—no matter what kind of work—if we're doing it with presence, we're practicing *tikkun olam*. It took me some time to realize that's what I was able to do with my role as funeral director, but once it clicked, suddenly the job seemed that much more important, that much more necessary for me to do.

There is a work of being present. There's a ministry of presence. And this ministry of presence is an embracing of the now, of the world, and of the earth. In some ways it's the work of a birth doula. Of waiting. Of listening. Of being a steady and small guide in the birth of life. It's not always doing work with large projects and plans and huge acts. Changing the world sometimes involves massive movements, but mostly it can be accomplished through small acts of presence, listening, and kindness. And I believe it starts with embracing the earth by keeping our minds and hearts here, and not yet in the beyond and the next life.

Somewhat reluctantly and somewhat because I had run out of money, I decided to go back to the Shire and join the funeral business. I no longer felt called to do things for the beyond. I was being called back to the earth, back to the mud, and back to Parkesburg to practice simple acts of being present. It was as though my DNA, my being, was tied to the earth of Parkesburg and as much as I thought the beyond was calling me outward, Parkesburg's earth was calling me home.

But my journey wouldn't be so simple.

7

THE MYTH OF THE
DEATH-CARE AMATEUR

Not long after I started working full-time at the funeral home, I received a call. "Wilde Funeral Home. Caleb speaking," I answered.

"Who?" the voice responded with a question that let me know the caller wasn't expecting to find my voice on the other end. This was a pretty typical reply for the first couple years I worked at the funeral home, so I learned to provide some context.

"This is Caleb Wilde." I made sure I gave my last name so that the caller knew where to place me. "I'm Bud's grandson. Bill's son."

"Oh, okay," the youngish fortysomething voice replied. "I'm looking for Bud."

"He's here. May I ask who's calling?"

"This is Tommy Ricci. The doctors are giving me two days to live. I'm bedridden at my house, and I was wondering if your grandpa could come visit me before I die."

I was a little taken aback. *How is a man two days away from his death talking this coherently?* was my first thought. I paused as the thought sunk in, and I eventually spit out, "Just a minute, let me get him for you."

I walked to the back room where I found my grandfather asleep in his La-Z-Boy. He typically looks like a dead man when he sleeps, with his face utterly relaxed, his mouth wide open, and the whites of his eyes peeking through his semiopen eyelids. I'm all too afraid that one day I will try to wake him up and find him unresponsive. Not this time. He woke up. I gave him a minute to gather himself, explained who was on the phone and why he was calling, and handed him the portable.

Tommy is just like most of the people Pop-Pop knows—a random acquaintance that my grandfather magically turned into a friend. I shouldn't say "magically" because it's art . . . an art that "Bud" has mastered. The way his friendliness comes naturally has always intimidated me and my introverted personality because I know I'll never be able to fill his shoes. I'm like an old cell-phone battery that needs five hours to charge for thirty minutes of usage. He's like a Timex watch. His smile calms a thousand questions, mine—sometimes forced—can create a thousand. I've had to learn to be social, but the act itself sucks the energy out of me. In a business where social funeral directors do well, I've managed to just barely keep my head above the ground.

Wherever Pop-Pop goes, he makes friends. And Tommy was no exception. Pop-Pop is a former chief for Parkesburg's fire company, and Tommy, a firefighter for a neighboring company, met Pop-Pop at an event where they clicked over bad jokes and even worse drinks.

The next day Pop-Pop fulfilled Tommy's last dying wish. When he got back from Tommy's house, I asked, "How was that?"

"He didn't want to talk about his funeral . . . he just wanted to give me a few new jokes to use for the next firemen's banquet. He looks better than his jokes. He'll last to New Year's."

Pop-Pop was wrong. Doctors are as good at death prediction as meteorologists are at weather forecasts, but Tommy's doctor saw the writing in the sky pretty clearly. Two days later, at about 1 P.M., on the eve of Christmas Eve, Tommy died. The family called, and they told us to wait because a couple of family members and friends wanted to see Tommy before we came. We waited and waited until 4 P.M. Then we called again to ask if they were ready for us to come pick him up. Pop-Pop was anxious to get to the Riccis' house, not because he wanted to push the family to hurry up but because he loves doing his work.

This time they said, "Tommy's uncle is coming from Norristown, an hour away. We want to wait for him." But Pop-Pop didn't want to wait at the funeral home, so we loaded the removal wagon and off we drove to Tommy's house. When we arrived, we found that the family had draped black linen across the front door. A sign was hung over the ribbon with this announcement scribbled in child's handwriting: "Dad died. Come on in if you want to see him."

We entered the house, and the whole of it stunk of cancer, a humid, thick, grainy stench. Tommy was lying on a hospice bed, set right in the middle of the living room, an intentional setup that was a statement about his last stage of life. While many hospice beds are hidden away back in a bedroom for privacy's sake, Tommy had his placed right in the house's heart of action, where he could visit with his close-knit friends, the neighbors he had adopted as family, and his blood family who were all within a couple of miles of his house.

Tommy's wife, Amy, was sitting in the kitchen getting her hair done in anticipation of Tommy's funeral. The woman cutting Amy's hair immediately looked at us and asked bluntly, "Who are you?"

My grandfather answered, "We're the Wilde boys."

"Oh," she replied quickly, "I've had some of you in my time." I laughed.

"How's that spelled?" she continued. I asked her if she knew of Oscar Wilde or perhaps the actress Olivia, which she did. I told her we spell our name like that.

The house was a hive of activity. Tommy's three daughters ran around the home, sometimes watching TV, sometimes talking to the neighbors who would randomly pop in and out, and sometimes sitting beside Tommy and stroking his arm. Pop-Pop kept everybody entertained, hugging those he knew and those he didn't know, acting the way he always does in planned funerals. This little unplanned visitation was a throwback to times past, with Pop-Pop playing the role of community undertaker.

We sat there for over two hours as we waited for that uncle from Norristown to arrive. He finally came, claimed "bad traffic" for his being late, took another half hour with Tommy, and around 7 P.M. we asked Tommy's wife, three daughters, two sisters, and parents if they were ready for us to take him back to the funeral home.

One by one, each family member kissed Tommy on his face before we took him back to the funeral home. His parents kissed his forehead, Tommy's children kissed his cheeks, and his wife kissed him on his lips. After they were done with their good-byes, Pop-Pop and I walked out to the removal wagon to grab the stretcher.

Tommy had forged his way in life. He didn't mind questioning and breaking boundaries, and it seemed his family was not different. After we had pulled the stretcher out of the back, I asked Pop-Pop, "Do you think Tommy's family would want to dress his body for the viewing?" As I had been sitting on the couch, I thought that if any family would want to do it, it'd be this family.

DRESSING A LOVED ONE, caring for him or her after the person has passed away is a great example of what a good death, a positive narrative, looks like. Part of what contributes to and perpetuates the death negative culture we find ourselves in is that death care has become an industry that has told people, *This is beyond your capabilities to handle. Death is scary, messy, gross, sad. Let us take care of it for you.*

When the funeral industry professionalized death care and did away with the "community undertaker," it implicitly and legally made death amateurs of everyone else. With doctors having authority over dying, and funeral directors gaining authority over death, it created a culture of death virgins . . . people who have little experience and know-how when it comes to the end stage of life. The funeral industry is partially to blame for creating the "death professional"; after all, the industry has worked hard to secure our position by creating laws and educational requirements to make us at least seem like the exclusive practitioners of death care.

But it wasn't just capitalist undertakers who created this

professional and amateur divide. Part of the reason the funeral industry buried the community undertaker was because death doesn't jive with the modern American vision and those Americans who embrace it. Death questions our delusion of self-mastery. So let's just ignore it. Or better yet, let's find someone else to handle it.

Americans found a "win-win" situation by giving their dying and dead over to a willing nursing home industry, hospital care that stays death like an overdue pregnancy, and a funeral industry that happily disposes of our dead, all of which the American public pays loads of our money to have someone else handle. The death negative narrative is threaded into the soul of America, so we've created multiple groups of professionals to handle it, all of it.

Funeral directors are one of those groups. We perform the magical disappearing act when we take your body, embalm it, dress it, casket it, and "poof," we give you a sleeping corpse unscathed by the deterioration of decomposition. Cremation is no different. The body is whisked away and comes back in a small little box, with little to no family participation. This magic is modern and contributes to the death negative narrative because we never get to touch death, care for our dead, and love our dead.

The axiom is simple, although forgotten, or ignored: the more we practice death care, the less we fear death itself; the closer we become to our dead, the more we can embrace our own mortality. In much of the history of our world, people have been much closer to death. Today, our death negative narratives are so strong that we rarely transcend them. But sometimes—so very rarely—families, like the Ricci family, transcend the narrative for just a little and instead of being an audience to the funeral process, they take the active role, pulling away the magic and making death visible once again.

SOMETIMES FAMILIES WANT TO transcend the narrative as much as they can. They take death into their hands and decide they are the professionals. In fact, many Amish still dress and casket their loved ones. The funeral director will embalm the deceased and then the Amish family will take the body into their care. Some families will wash the deceased, then they'll gently clothe the deceased and place the body into the plain wooden casket. Many Mormons, Muslims, and Jews all do the same. This is one of the luxuries of a close-knit community, and it was a luxury I wanted to offer the Riccis.

Pop-Pop agreed. "Why don't you ask them," he said.

We rolled the stretcher through the front door, and walked it over to the bed where Tommy lay. Pop-Pop invited anyone who wanted to help lend a hand, and in a couple of seconds a good dozen people surrounded Tommy's bed; we grabbed the bed's mattress sheet, cocooned his body with it, and passed his body over to the stretcher. After Pop-Pop and I had strapped him on the stretcher, Pop-Pop confirmed the time we'd meet with them tomorrow for the funeral arrangements, instructed them to bring the clothing they wanted Tommy to wear for the viewing, and then Pop-Pop left the conversation open for my question.

I cleared my throat, not sure how they'd respond to what I was about to ask them. I said, "Would you guys be interested in dressing Tommy for his funeral?"

Tears started running down the face of Tommy's wife. His sisters started crying, too. Their love was looking for an outlet, and this was one way they could express it.

Amid the tears, they responded, "Could we?" And with my yes the wife embraced me and started sobbing on my shoulder. By the time she was done hugging me, I had joked that she'd have to pay to have her snot dry-cleaned off my suit.

I drove on the way back to the funeral home. As I was driving, my introverted tendencies were kicking in, and I started to question why I had just put thousands of miles on my Subaru and spent nearly four years of my life and a bunch of money to earn a professional degree to do something that those without it could mostly do all on their own. Before we left, Amy had said she wanted Tommy to be embalmed for a viewing and then cremated afterward. Sure, Tommy's family couldn't embalm, but they had just had their makeshift public viewing. And hell-no were they going to try DIY cremation, but their DIY viewing and visitation was a spontaneous thing of beauty. While Pop-Pop certainly helped in keeping everyone smiling and happy, they didn't need the all-powerful funeral professional to take their hand and guide them through the deep dark corridors of death. They were pretty comfortable with Tommy's dead body and seemed to want to do as much as they could on their own. As valuable as my funeral education had been, the old "community undertaker" model would have worked just fine for the Ricci family. The Riccis were no death-care amateurs.

The next day, Christmas Eve, the Riccis were at our front door, clothing in hand. They made the funeral arrangements with Pop-Pop, and when they were finished, I guided them to the dressing room while explaining how the process of dressing a dead body worked. "Grief brain" is like being drunk. It's hard to be "in the moment" as nearly 80 to 90 percent of your brain energy is being redirected to grasping the new normal of life after loss. I wasn't sure if Tommy's family's grief brain would keep them from being able to do the task at hand. Maybe they'd burst into tears and storm out of the dressing room. Maybe they wouldn't be able to stomach seeing the incision near his collarbone and would somehow hate me for cutting their loved one during embalming.

They walked into the dressing room with stoic faces, bent on completing the task at hand without being encumbered by the obvious emotional weight of the whole thing. We laid out the clothing and cut Tommy's undershirt, dress shirt, and sport

coat down the back. We used the body lifter to put his under-
wear, pants, and socks on. Then we tucked in the shirt, laced
the belt through his pants. One of the sisters combed his hair
and styled it. They all talked to him, just like I do when I'm
with bodies.

"Are your pants too tight? I'll loosen that belt . . . your favorite raggedy old belt," Amy said.

"Let me get your hair just how you liked it. You could be a
pompous thing with this hair of yours."

"I know you hated dressing up, but you have a big day
coming, gonna see a lot of people."

And finally, "I love you, Tom. See ya in a few."

On the day of the service, all of Tommy's family and over
two hundred other people showed up to the church. It was a
few days after Christmas, and the church was still dressed in
its Advent outfitting. Wreaths and candles filled the air with
holiday scents, and the cheer that seeps into this special time of
year had seeped into the hearts of those who filled the church.

Because life is this beautiful, complex, and messy web of
giving ourselves away to others, and allowing others to give
themselves to us, shouldn't our dying process be supported by
those who created our web of life? Shouldn't our death be supported not by a single funeral home or funeral director, but by
these life connections that have been created by us and those
that have created us? Funeral directors hold incredible value—
and we've always existed in one form or another—because

death is hard, but I believe bereaved families are robbing themselves and our loved ones by capitulating dying and death over to the "experts."

Tommy's family taught me that anyone can—and should—be a part of the death-care process. And I'm sorry our sometimes-capitalist intentions have made people "amateurs." I'm sorry that we've helped create the death negative narrative by monopolizing death care, but I think together, in the messiness of life and death, we can find a way to grow closer to our dying and our dead. We can find the life in death.

8

FRONT-DOOR POLICY

A nother area of the death-care industry that I interact with often is the nursing home, and when someone dies at a nursing home, the process of removing the deceased has a certain degree of awkwardness. At night, there are no visitors at the nursing home, and most of the residents are sleeping, so the nursing staff just lets us go down the hallways uninhibited. During the day, because of nursing home visitors and residents wandering the halls, most nursing staff go into "hide the corpse" mode.

Funeral directors making a removal at a nursing home generally use the back door that is located out of sight from the residents, what we call the "back-door policy." There's usually a little call phone at the back door. We pick it up, get a hold of the front desk, and say something to the effect of, "This is Caleb Wilde with the Wilde Funeral Home here to pick up Ms. So-and-So. I'm at the back door. Can you have someone let me in?"

Within a couple minutes, a smiling nurse opens up the door to let us in. The nurse will close every resident's door that lines the path from the back door to the room where the deceased resides. All the nurses work together to herd the residents to areas where they won't see me and what I'm about to do. We sneak through the halls like ninjas, hoping no one sees that someone at a nursing home has actually died.

Hospitals have the "hide the corpse" method down to a science. Nearly every hospital has a morgue to house the deceased so that they're out of sight. In a sense, a death to the hospital is like an atheist to the church. It's that gnawing reminder that this facility, this institution doesn't have all the answers to all the world's health problems. So they ostracize the deceased to a cold little room in the back and hope that no one notices. Perhaps there's no place where the death negative narrative has a greater hold than within the walls of a hospital.

This secretive way we handle death and dying is relatively new. Up until the late 1800s, doctors would visit the deceased's home, and even the funeral directors would do their work at the deceased's home. My grandfather still remembers embalming in other people's homes on occasion when he was a teenager. They'd carry the portable gravity embalmer, mix the fluid in the flask, and raise the flask at the appropriate height to achieve the desired fluid pressure. He and his dad would play a game to see who could spill the least blood on the deceased's kitchen floor. When they weren't embalming in other people's kitchens, they would embalm in the funeral home's kitchen. They'd pull out the embalming table and let the blood drain into the kitchen sink. In 1954, Great-Mom-Mom Wilde got her wish, and we finally added a morgue to the funeral home, keeping the dead out of her kitchen.

Even then, until we bought the funeral home in 1928, all the viewings took place in the deceased's parlor room, and the funeral took place in a church.

In the modern world, where dying has been taken out of the home and community and moved into the hospital, the doctor has replaced community as the authoritative center. We've accepted this transition from community to medical authority for good reason. Doctors, hospitals, and nursing homes provide miraculous care of the body. But when those miracles run empty, death becomes the iconoclast, tearing down the perception that medicine can solve it all.

I understand the tension that hospitals and nursing homes have when someone dies. People believe that medical science can do the miraculous, but when inevitability comes, it dashes our hope in these miracles. Instead of poking holes in our faith in medicine, we keep death out of sight, hiding the evidence, for fear it will be disheartening to the hospital occupants and their visitors.

Elisabeth Kübler-Ross writes about the invisible death in this way:

Dying is an integral part of life, as natural and predictable as being born. But whereas birth is cause for celebration, death has become a dreaded and unspeakable issue to be avoided by every means possible in our modern society. . . . It is difficult to accept death in this society because it is unfamiliar. In spite of the fact that it happens all the time, we never see it. When a person dies in a hospital, he is quickly whisked away; a magical disappearing act does away with the evidence before it could upset anyone.[1]

I've always thought there must be a better way to deal with death than the "disappearing act" of the back-door policy. There must be a way that allows us to honor death instead of hide it. There must be a way that allows us to embrace death instead of mask it. And then the other day, I finally had a chance to experience it done another way.

IT HAPPENED DURING THE busiest time we've ever had at the funeral home. On that specific day, we had three services: one in the morning, one in the afternoon, and one in the evening. I had worked all three and was just getting ready to go home around 8 P.M. when my phone rang. It was a call from Luther Acres Nursing Home in Lititz. I jumped in the van and drove an hour to Lititz.

My record of working a combination of funerals and removals is thirty hours straight. This call, although thankfully not close to the thirty-hour record, was going to give me a solid fourteen-hour day. After I was done, I'd go home, sleep, then wake up and do it all again the next day. We were so busy it was like we were living in our suits.

I had never been to Luther Acres so I called the nursing station when I was about ten minutes out.

"Hi. This is Caleb Wilde from the funeral home. I'm coming to pick up Mrs. Taylor," I said. "I'm close to the nursing home. Where do you want me to go?"

I expected the nurse to give some detailed directions about how I was to drive behind the home, look for the back door, and use the call phone, and so on, but instead, she replied cheerfully, "We have a front-door policy. Just pull up to the main entrance."

I could feel the stress drain from my body. I didn't really know what she meant by "front-door policy," but she sounded so cheerful saying it that I figured it had to be something positive.

Ten minutes later I pulled my van up to the front door. The

nurse was waiting outside to greet me, which rarely happens. Instead of sneaking me through as I was used to, she led me through the front doors, down the hall, and into Mrs. Taylor's room. Mrs. Taylor's family had already come and gone so it was just the nurse and me in the room with Mrs. Taylor.

As I transferred Mrs. Taylor from her bed to my stretcher, I asked the nurse some questions about Mrs. Taylor to get a feel for the nurse's relationship with the deceased. Questions such as:

"How long has she been here?"

"Has she suffered the last couple days?"

"Was she verbal?"

It's presumptuous to think that nurses don't grieve the losses of their residents. Many of these residents have been at the nursing homes for years. Many of them love their nurses. And many of the nurses develop a friendship with those they care for on a daily basis.

But that wasn't the case with Mrs. Taylor. She was in late-stage dementia when she entered the nursing home and a friendship wasn't a possibility. But I've seen how love can exist in a relationship that seems like a one-way street. Just like we have an innate connection with and compassion for babies, we also have an innate connection with and compassion for the aging and the disabled.

Sacred is a word that we need to reclaim. It has lost its meaning because we associate the word with religious connotations—something is only sacred if it has been sanctified by religion. It's a definition that works in some cases, but beyond the religious connection, sacredness is defined by love. When something or someone is loved, that love sanctifies it. Our children are sacred. Our loved ones are sacred. Our hobbies are sacred. And our aging and disabled loved ones are sacred because they are loved. Even our dead are sacred because though the body no longer works, it is still sanctified by the love of family and friends.

What followed next at Luther Acres was one of the most sacred acts I've seen in my short life.

After I had finished transferring Mrs. Taylor onto my stretcher, the nurse pulled out an "honor quilt" that the staff had made. She helped me drape the quilt over the stretcher, explaining that it signified wrapping the body in the love and care of the staff. Then she said, "Wait here. I'll be right back."

After a couple minutes of waiting she finally came back.

"Okay," she said. "We do an honor walk here. Our staff forms a line along the walls of the nursing home, from here to the entrance," she explained. "You'll take Mrs. Taylor and just roll out to your van."

"Do you do this for everyone?" I asked in amazement.

"Day or night," she said.

I thought about what it must look like during the day when the nursing home is buzzing with visitors and residents. I thought about how it would literally mean that for a couple minutes, the work of the nursing home would stop as all the staff lined the hall for the walk. This wasn't hiding death, or making death invisible. This was honoring a deceased resident. This was embracing death. This was right. This was sacred.

I walked through the doorway and into the hall with Mrs. Taylor loaded on my stretcher. I was flanked on either side by the nursing staff. They stood in silence, honoring Mrs. Taylor. I felt honored, too. Because it wasn't just Mrs. Taylor that they were acknowledging; in an indirect way, they were acknowledging me. They were acknowledging my work and my profession in a profoundly special way. I was at the end of a fourteen-hour day, but I felt rejuvenated. I didn't feel like I needed to be hidden. I didn't feel invisible.

Everything felt right when I loaded Mrs. Taylor into the back of my van. My day had been long. I was tired. But Luther Acres had honored Mrs. Taylor. They had recognized their own grief. They had recognized the loss of one of their residents. They even acknowledged me. They had recognized death and they had done something incredibly sacred.

9

LISTENING TO THE
VOICE OF SILENCE

Even as a young man working at the funeral home, I still found myself using my religion as a way to manufacture a form of anxiety management. I wanted principle, I wanted certainty, and I wanted the universal truth. I wanted to box God and use God as the cornerstone in my bulwark against the chaos of death. Religion had become my existential narcotic, my immortality project of choice, all of which was challenged a couple of years ago as I watched the faces of Robbie's children.

I PICKED UP THE phone with my rehearsed greeting. The woman's voice on the other end said abruptly, "I have a problem . . . my son-in-law Robbie was killed in a motorcycle accident yesterday."

Now that I knew the nature of her call, the next five or six sentences were as rehearsed as the first.

"I'm so sorry for your loss."

"Thank you," she said.

I paused, waiting to see if the silence elicited any further response; and, at the same time, I'm contemplating if I should deviate from the script and ask her about the details of the death.

Keeping with the script, I continue, inquiring about the hospital he's at, the name of her daughter (Jenna), her daughter's phone number, and then the hardest question of them all.

"Do you know if Jenna wants embalming or cremation?" I said with hesitation.

And what proceeded was her only scripted response.

"It depends on the condition of his body. The coroner told us he slammed into a tree without his helmet on, but they wouldn't tell us any more. If he's bad . . . cremation. If he's fixable . . . embalming."

We then went over the plan of action, which consisted of me calling the hospital to see if her son-in-law was released, calling the coroner to inquire about the condition of the body, and then calling her back to let her know a time she could come into the funeral home and make funeral arrangements.

I called the coroner.

Got the release from the hospital.

And an hour later I was standing in the morgue unzipping the body bag to see if the body of this forty-year-old man was viewable. It was the back of the head that was crushed by the tree, something we could piece back together for his wife and four young children (ages five to thirteen), so they could see their husband and daddy one last time.

After a total of about ten man-hours of stitching, gluing, filling, and applying makeup, his head still didn't look right. Dead people never look right. We're so used to seeing them alive that dead is never accurate, but this was different. This was a motorcycle accident that threw a man's head into a tree. This was like piecing together one of Gallagher's watermelons.

We gave the wife a choice to continue with the public viewing or close the lid and she chose to keep it open, sharing the reality and source of her pain in all its distortion, even sharing it with her four young children and all their schoolmates that came to the funeral in support, many of whom saw unperfected death for the very first time.

The scheduled end of the viewing came and went, but people kept coming to view. Large viewings like Robbie's usually have one of the following factors. First, connections. If the deceased is well connected, is an active member of a church or an active member of the community, or simply has a large family, a funeral will likely be large. A second factor is age. The younger the person at death, the larger the funeral. But one of the greatest indicators of the size of a viewing is the type of death.

Tragic deaths almost always create large funerals, and I'm not entirely sure why. Pop-Pop's theory is that tragic deaths bring out the gawkers who, even though they have minimal acquaintance to the family of the deceased, have maximum curiosity to see just how messed up the deceased looks. I like to look at the brighter side. My theory is that people just feel more deeply for tragedy and are more likely to want to show up. Whatever the reason, Robbie's funeral had a little bit of all these large funeral factors, so much so that the viewing went an hour past the scheduled end. Finally, the last person filed past the casket and the family knew their time to say their last good-bye had come.

The viewing was held in a small church, with the casket positioned at the front of a full sanctuary. As a way to provide privacy to the family, we turned the open casket around so that the open lid blocked the view from the pews, creating a private space where tears could be shed in their honest shock.

The well-designed acoustics of this sanctuary were meant for singing praise, but today they resounded with the cries of four children and their mother, making time stand still. Until the grandfather came up to the casket, wrapped his arms around the children, and said, "This is hard for you to understand."

As the sanctuary reverberated with the cries produced by an inexplicable death, there wasn't a person in the room who understood.

All tried to understand. All grasped for an explanation.

In this moment—as I watched these young children—I became like them. With all the well-intended clichés emptied of meaning, I allowed my mind to reconcile with what my heart was telling me: *I simply can't understand something that doesn't make sense.*

There's no "higher plan" in Robbie's death.

Time will not heal all these wounds.

God doesn't need another angel in heaven.

FOR MOST OF MY teenage and adult life, I've searched for answers that would satisfy my anxiety. My "monk years" in high school, my time pursuing degrees in seminary, and even my current academic pursuit are an attempt to find the right words. I've gathered a lot of words to combat the quiet. The concept of God has been my *deus ex machina,* that plot device I've dropped down from the heavens to solve the most difficult of experiences. But for the first time in my life, at Robbie's funeral, I allowed the silence to creep into my being and accepted that while ideas of heaven and resurrection may have value for some, right now, right here as we closed the lid of Robbie's casket, I couldn't believe that those answers fully satisfied the cries of Robbie's children.

As I watched the lid close, I knew that I had to embrace the Holy Saturday, that sacred day in the Christian calendar when we worship in doubt, uncertainty, and the feeling of abandonment. I knew that I had to allow death to topple my immortality projects so that I could approach death honestly. Looking back, it wasn't that I lost my faith (although at the time I thought that might be the case), but rather that my faith was being quieted. It was as though God looked at me and whispered, "Shhhhh."

It reminded me of what I once read about World War I. Britain's Remembrance Day was first commemorated on November 11, 1919, in honor of the dead of World War I. In its November 12, 1919, edition, the *Manchester Guardian* described the day as such: "The first stroke of eleven produced a magical effect. The tram cars glided into stillness, motors ceased to cough and fume and stopped dead, and the mighty-limbed dray horses hunched back upon their loads and stopped also, seeming to do it on their own volition. . . . Everyone stood very still. The hush deepened. It had spread over the whole city and become so pronounced as to impress one with a sense of audibility. It was a silence which was almost pain . . . and the spirit of memory brooded over it all."

The silence of death is often painful because it exposes our most basic fear. It lays bare the fact that our best answers, our best immortality projects, and our best forms of death denial aren't good enough for the cries of Robbie's children. Our brain has biologically wired us to forecast the future, which makes us crave certainty as a survival method, and we almost have to short-circuit our brain to listen to death. David Rock, cofounder of the NeuroLeadership Institute, wrote:

> The brain likes to know the pattern occurring moment to moment; it craves certainty, so that prediction is possible. Without prediction, the brain must use dramatically more resources, involving the more energy-intensive prefrontal cortex, to process moment-to-moment experience. Even a small amount of uncertainty generates an "error" response in the orbital frontal cortex. This takes attention away from one's goals, forcing attention to the error. . . . Larger uncertainties, like not knowing your boss's expectations or if your job is secure, can be highly debilitating.[1]

This is why the instability that comes with the loss of a loved one can wreck our lives. It sucks away all our brain's energy and directs it to reestablishing a sense of stability.

This is why traumatic events can ruin a child's school performance.

This is why a divorce can hurt a person's ability to accomplish tasks at work.

This is why one tragic death can destroy a whole family.

This is why we so crave truth tellers, religious leaders, economic forecasters, and political pundits who give us a sense of certainty. We're only satisfied when it feels like we have sufficient explanations and certainties. But in silence, we have to consciously deny our survival instinct and biological wiring and acknowledge that our answers, our explanations, our certainties, our immortality projects may not fulfill our questions, doubts, and uncertainty. In fact, the lack of certainty lays a foundation for fear. Perhaps our fear of death is because there's such a lack of certainty in the wake of its silence. Perhaps we fear the silence just as much as we fear death. Perhaps we fear silence more than death.

To become comfortable in silence may be the first step in becoming comfortable with death because, on the most basic biological level, death and silence are the same. Conversely, being comfortable in the silence may be the first step in pursuing life. As I would come to learn, death may not be so horrible after all. In fact, death may be the most beautiful thing about this human experiment. But I believe we can only see the positive in death when we learn to accept the silence. When we're able to tap that reservoir of bravery and lay aside all our words against death, and sit, not as the teacher of death, but as the student, listening to what death has to say in the silence, this is the first step.

It's not an easy step, though, as I would soon find out.

10

GRIEF AS WORSHIP

I was about a year in as a licensed funeral director, helping my grandfather dress an older man for his viewing. I'd been assisting Pop-Pop in the prep room and morgue as soon as Pennsylvania granted me the status of "apprentice funeral director," helping him with everything from embalming to cosmetics to casketing. I knew how long Pop-Pop wanted his suture strings cut, how he liked his embalming instruments laid out, and where he liked the surgical lamp placed during the different stages of his embalming process. Embalming affords a mistake or two, as there's usually other options that can be explored if the first option doesn't work, but dressing a body is not always so gracious.

Some funeral directors attempt to put clothing on a dead body the way you and I put our clothes on in the morning, but most of us cut through the back of the shirt or dress and slip it on as you would a hospital gown. Cutting through the back also allows us to fit the shirt to the deceased's current weight, which has usually fluctuated up or down depending on the nature of the person's death. The cutting of clothing is a serious business because one small lapse of concentration and there's no going back. We don't have music playing in the background when we're embalming, and—especially when we're dressing—we rarely talk, because we're quietly focusing on the task and details at hand, making sure all our mental energy is present as we do our dressing dance. Sometimes, though, we break the sacred silence.

I was fitting a man's shirt to his thinned-out neck when we heard the phone ring and my dad, who was in the nearby office, answer it. When you've been around death long enough, you find there can be, at times, a rhythm to it. For instance, the Pennsylvania winter often brings the flu season, pneumonia, and other such ailments that push those who are just about ready to die over the life limit. We were in that season and so when the phone rang, I blurted out prophetically, "It's a death call." My grandfather rejoined, "What's his name?" I walked out of the morgue, over and into the office, to see my dad scribbling down "Chad"; I promptly returned and, to my grandfather's astonishment, told him the name of the person who had just passed. Unfortunately, though, this was not an older man whose last straw had been pulled by the flu season. This was a young man who had been overcome by his drug addiction in a seedy hotel.

I walked to the garage and pulled out our late '90s Buick conversion wagon, put our stretcher in the back, and grabbed some latex gloves and protective wear, remembering back to a couple months ago when I pulled another person who had overdosed out of a third-floor hotel room. That hotel didn't have an elevator, so my dad and I shouldered the loaded stretcher down the stairs, and due to the tight quarters of the hotel and the way the guy died, we took a huge risk and lugged the dead man headfirst down the stairs, prompting him to discharge the contents of his stomach all over my clothing, an experience I vowed would never be repeated.

After driving about a half hour, we pulled up to the one-story hotel; I breathed a sigh of relief. The police let us past the tape and showed us to the room where we saw Chad's body lying with a white cloth draped over him. "Careful when you lift him," they warned us, "there may be needles under his body."

There was drug paraphernalia lying around the hotel room that he apparently called home. We wheeled our stretcher over to where Chad was lying and pulled back the white blanket covering his body to find a discolored, half-naked, late-twentysomething man lying faceup with what appeared to be water resting in the crevice between his closed eyelid and his nose. I didn't know if it was water, saliva, or tears; many of these cases provide small puzzle pieces to the deceased's last minutes of life, but rarely are there enough pieces to create the whole, leaving the rest to our imagination. Maybe Chad cried as he realized his impending fate, or maybe he fell and spilled a cup of water on his face, or maybe it was a small puddle of sweat his body produced from the drugs raising his heart rate and blood pressure. Whatever it was, there was still a job to be done, so we slid him over onto the stretcher, wheeled him into the wagon, took him back to the funeral home, and embalmed him.

On the morning of the funeral, we arrived at the church an hour or so early to set up and prepare. We like to be the first ones at a church funeral, but today we were beat by Chad's mother, who was setting photos of her son around the small sanctuary of the church with a smile on her face. She had photos of Chad as an infant, dressed in his baby clothes; the classic T-ball photo shoots that are equal parts Americana and boyhood dreams; the prom photo shoot; the graduate photos. And that was it. The pictures stopped after high school when he decided to pursue a life away from his parents.

I took note of Chad's mother's smile as I was setting up the flowers around the casket, and I asked her how she was doing. This all-too-common and easy question is fully loaded at a funeral. If I'm honest, it's a question I should strike altogether from my funeral vernacular. It's no surprise when someone responds, "I'm at a funeral, how do you think I'm doing?" But her response has stuck with me. She said, "I've never slept so good in ten years. There is something worse than death; there's staying up night after night worrying about the whereabouts and well-being of a son who is controlled by addiction. He's resting in peace and so am I."

Soon after we had everything set up, people started coming into the sanctuary to view Chad and visit with his family. When a young person dies suddenly, viewings have the tendency to be large and long, but not so much with those who have overdosed. Drugs can have an isolating effect on the social lives of addicts, causing smaller and sometimes gloomy viewings and funerals, but that was not the case for Chad's viewing. Even though his drug addiction had taken his life, it didn't stop him from living, as the viewing line went well past the advertised 2:00 P.M. close of the viewing, pushing up to the 2:30 mark. At 2:30, we started to gather the family together for the closing of the lid when one of Chad's friends scurried up to us. "There's a friend that needs to see Chad before you shut the lid . . . he's two minutes away," he pleaded. The family agreed to wait. Two minutes turned into ten minutes and ten to twenty, and still no sign of the friend. We never want to push the family by saying, "It's been twenty minutes and it's time to get started," but at the same time, funeral directors live in the tension of being sensitive funeral servants and decisive funeral directors. I suggested, "Can you call your friend on his cell phone to see where he's at?"

Just about that time, the friend came through the door, saving me from having to be the time-conscious funeral director. He didn't come on his initiative; he was being pushed up to the casket, maybe even pulled up, by a couple of his friends. And he was resisting their force just enough to let his pushing and pulling friends know that he didn't want to view the body, but not enough to totally resist their insistence. As he got closer to the casket, his body was facing the coffin, but his head was turned away, jaw tightly shut in defiance and fists clenched as though he was ready for a fight. He *was* fighting. Fighting loss. Fighting fear. Maybe fighting his shame. He was fighting until he got to the casket, saw his friend, and forfeited his battle. The clenched fists opened and started touching his dead friend's chest; his head that was turned away was now fixated on the face of his deceased friend. His tightly shut jaw was now open, gasping for air as his body was shaking. Then he started to weep. Tears are like a good confession. His body collapsed onto Chad's, and what had been fighting denial now became a full embrace.

Crying at funerals is contagious. The casket was positioned at the front of the nearly full sanctuary so that this whole unfolding drama was on display for all who were watching. As soon as his unreserved cries started, everyone else was wiping their eyes, grabbing for tissues, and embracing their pew neighbors. Tears consumed the attendees, ushering a sense of the sacred into the sanctuary.

I believe there's a place hidden inside humans that hasn't been wounded by shame and fear. A place where there's still innocence, where we haven't been calloused by the friction of hurt. A place so innocent that we can be ourselves, in all our messiness and peculiarity, and still believe that we'll be loved. It's a place where there's no need to put up fronts of perfection and wholeness, no need to paint our faces and cover our flaws. That place is often exposed by death. We picture death's hand as cold, capricious bone when it may be the hand of an expert clockmaker, able to turn and fix those intricate parts that still harbor a sense of Eden, where vulnerability is normal, and shame has little power. At Chad's funeral, Eden had been rediscovered. No one was looking at their cell phones. No one was preoccupied with what they had done that morning or what they had to do afterward. In one beautiful moment, everyone was present and shame free. Because sometimes when it seems like everything is falling apart, we're actually coming together.

After everyone was seated, the pastor stepped up to the pulpit, seemingly unmoved by the moment. Like me, he was probably thinking about the logistics of starting the funeral later than advertised. Thoughts like *Should I cut the sermon short? What part should I trim?* were probably running through his mind. I have sympathy for pastors because their lives and jobs often mirror mine—the fluid, unscheduled hours, the drama; pastors too are often on the front lines of death care. I've seen pastors clean up suicide scenes, picking skull fragments out of a bathroom ceiling, I've seen pastors sit up late nights at the bedside of the dying, and I've seen them hold family members as they say their last good-bye as the casket lid closes. Despite my admiration, however, I had little sympathy for what this pastor was about to say. Much of our death negative narrative is shaped by these funeral sermons, and I had become sensitive to narratives that were detrimental to our view of death.

"We know why we're here," he bellowed. "Just like the Bible says: 'The wages of sin *is* death,'" he said emphatically, as he managed to cast us all out of Eden with two sentences. "We all sin and fall short of God's glory and we will all die because that is our punishment for Adam's sin, but Chad's sin directly led to his death." I looked around the room and watched Chad's friends turn their heads down. The pastor assumed that Chad's friends shared in Chad's lifestyle. The people at funerals are a reflection of the deceased, and since Chad's life involved drugs, the pastor's assumption probably wasn't too far off.

I'VE QUESTIONED THIS "death as punishment" narrative for years. It finds its roots in the Garden of Eden story where death is the inherited punishment for the sin of Adam and Eve or in the phrase used by St. Paul, "the wages of sin is death." Here, death is no longer a natural part of nature, a way nature makes room for the next generation, but an imposed consequence. In this narrative, our mortal needs and sin are too often confused one for the other. In this narrative, death is something to be feared, something to be fought against, and something to be hidden. All of which leads to a deeply ingrained mortality shaming and a deeply damaging implication that we will never be enough in this life unless we try, try, try to be more than a mortal, by the grace of God.

I had begun to see that if I rejected the death negative narrative, I also needed to reject mortality shaming and the "you will never be enough" story. I had learned that accepting myself, not as inherently sinful, but as inherently mortal is acknowledging that my fears about death, my insecurity, my hunger, my tiredness, the wearing out of my body, my sexuality, my need for others, my growing older, these parts of my mortality that I can sometimes alternately loathe and celebrate, they—all of them—don't deserve the shame I often place on them. Because being inherently mortal doesn't mean we're inherently sinful.

Letting go of this shame has allowed for vulnerability in my life. There have been times that I've been weak, that I've fallen hard, that I've ridden in the back of an ambulance because I was burned out by death. There were times when I allowed my mortality to be the occasion to be selfish and fearful. There were times when I was not enough. But I reached out to others because I wasn't ashamed by my mortality.

With this mortality positivity and lack of shame, I have become more willing to acknowledge that I need other people to help me. I am able to acknowledge that I am growing and that I can learn from others. For me, vulnerability isn't giving into shame and acting like I have it all together because I don't. Vulnerability isn't acting like I can do it all by myself because I can't. Vulnerability is being honest with where I'm at and grabbing the hands of those who can guide me, and being shameless enough to admit my problems to them. Chad had an addiction, but maybe the message that Chad and some of his other friends needed to hear that day was that they aren't inherently wrong, they are inherently mortal, and there's no need to feel shame about it. The first step toward breaking free of our problems is acknowledging that we all need help, we all need love, we all need each other, we all need healing, and we must find healthier ways to meet our needs. After all, whatever reason prompts drug use—whether it be to mask pain, to escape a difficult life, to feel included, to feel pleasure, or to feed an addiction—all these things strike at the very heart of what it means to be human.

I WAS STANDING IN the back of the sanctuary, keeping my eyes zeroed in on the friend we had all waited for and who had just wept on Chad's chest. He was clearly agitated. The pastor's body language communicated strength, with his chest puffed ever so slightly, his stern voice lowered. The pastor's language wasn't aimed at Chad's friends, but it was the language of his seminary, interspersed with theological verbiage and words that let everyone know he was the authority in the room. He continued, "But God, in God's wise plan, ordained us to be here today. Even though we don't understand his plan, God remains strong and unmoved."

While Chad's friends bowed their heads in shame as the preacher waxed on, there was another segment of people in the crowd who, like the pastor himself, held their heads up high like peacocks. As the pastor talked about God's perfection and our sinfulness, they acted like they had almost transcended their mortality by acting like—in the pastor's words—this "strong and unmoved" version of God. They painted their faces to look like their imagined image of God. They weren't vulnerable though. I certainly couldn't read their minds, but with this group that gave nods of approval and whispered "amen" to the pastor's message, it was almost like they had achieved this transcendence, that through the power of thought, ethics, or God, they were no longer weak, interdependent, and vulnerable— no longer mortal.

But I think the problem goes deeper, especially with those who claim to be religious. The problem has something to do with our view of God as the ultimate of mortality transcendence. There's this picture of God that paints God as having no need, a God who is immortal, who isn't dependent on others, and who can stand alone unhurt and untouched by relationships. In a word, God has no vulnerability, or so we think. Like the peacocks and the pastor at Chad's funeral, we try to imitate the God we believe in.

So many religious traditions, especially the narratives I have too often heard at funerals, believe that God is unable to change and is unaffected by emotion because, they suppose, change and emotions are signs of weakness. Should it be a surprise that so many of "God's people" become unmoved and emotionally repressed? Should it be a surprise that sometimes God's people try to be so stoic and emotionless about grief and death? So many of us (and this is me more than I care to admit) resist grief, resist joy, resist sadness, because the One we worship, the One we are trying to reflect has no emotion in Godself.

If the problem of mortality shaming flows from a view of God as "perfect," wouldn't it be interesting if the narrative was turned on its head and instead of a "perfect" God, we talked about a God who was vulnerable? Wouldn't it be interesting if vulnerability lies at the very core of God? If we shared *this* view of God around death and funerals, Chad's friends might not have held their heads in shame, but maybe they could have found community. If the pastor could have talked about a God who stands, maybe even kneels, with us in weakness and vulnerability, maybe they would have found God.

If God is really love, if God sees us and feels with us, it means that at God's core is this vulnerability, an interdependence that allows God to feel our pains, to know our sorrows and our joys. Maybe it's okay to have sorrow. Maybe it's okay to weep. It's okay to be vulnerable, for when we do so, we aren't becoming unlike God, we are, in fact, worshipping.

I never found out the backstory of Chad's late-arriving friend. I don't know why he struggled so much to see Chad. I can speculate that this friend was Chad's best friend. Maybe he was there when Chad overdosed. Maybe they were roommates in that little hotel room. I do know one thing: on that day of Chad's funeral, this grieving friend of Chad's worshipped so genuinely that for a few brief moments he led the entire room back into Eden.

11

SARA'S MOSAIC

I t was six in the morning.

My grandfather and I drove up to the house, and an uncle of the deceased was standing outside with a cigarette in hand, ready to meet us and guide us into the house.

"You guys are here for my niece, Sara."

He took a deep drag from his half-smoked cigarette, blew smoke into the crisp morning air, and explained that Sara was eight years old and had been fighting cancer for four years.

"She's in the living room with her mother, Joan. Follow me," he said.

We entered the house, walked into the living room, where about twenty family members and friends were scattered all over—some sitting, and some standing, others lying on the floor. Some of the people in this room were connected not by blood, but by the progressive growth of abnormal cells and the shared struggle those cells create. Cancer has a way of creating a hodgepodge community that isn't connected by church or sports or club memberships, but by struggle, pain, and chance meetings in children's hospitals.

My grandfather made his way around the room hugging all who were willing. And I took the logistical job of surveying the room and determining how we were going to do our job of wheeling a stretcher into this people-packed space and removing Sara back to the van. As I surveyed, I noticed a very startling fact: I didn't see Sara.

When a terminal person is dying under home hospice care, as Sara had, sometimes hospice sets up the temporary hospital bed in the living room of the first floor, enabling larger groups to visit the dying. It's the little things that hospice does that make death and dying a little graceful, especially for us funeral directors and our backs. Having people die on the first floor is so much easier than having them die like Jack McClure, who had the nerve to pass away in his sixth-floor apartment on the exact day the elevator was being repaired.

Although Sara's bed was set up in the living room, she wasn't lying on it.

Unlike some families, who just want us to come to the house, take away their dead, and do our job, Sara's family and friends wanted to explain to us who Sara was, what she meant to them. It was important for them to tell the stories, to believe that through their stories of Sara—concise as they were at 6 A.M.—she could be incarnated in us so that we could love her, too, and become proxy family. They told us how she'd encourage her fellow cancer patients at the hospital, making them cards and always sharing her beloved Hershey Kisses. How she'd always manage to find a smile even in the darkest of times. They talked about her desire to die at home and how, in her final days, she was even concerned about her family's ability to cope after she died. There was something endearing about the way they told the stories, about how they talked about Sara, and about how real they made her feel to us, complete strangers.

After listening to their stories, absorbing them, we asked them if they were ready for us to make our removal. They confirmed that they had all said their good-byes.

And then I asked the obvious question, "Where is Sara?"

"She's here," said Joan, Sara's mother. And then we saw her. Joan was holding a small girl who looked to be around five years old with a knit beanie on her head. Because it was so early in the morning, we had just assumed that one of Sara's younger sisters had fallen asleep in Joan's arms. Because Sara was wearing a hat, we didn't see her chemo-induced hair loss.

It turned out that Sara had died in her mother's arms, and there she lay, a small pile of bones, large enough to fill a whole room with this group of people.

As if Sara were simply a sleeping child, my grandfather got down on his knees, slid his arms under Sara's head and thighs, lifted her body out of her mother's lap, and carried her to our stretcher.

There is a difference between empathy and sympathy and it is an important distinction for those who work in caregiving. Dr. Nicola Davies writes on her website, "Imagine being at the bottom of a deep, dark hole. Peer up to the top of the hole and you might see some of your friends and family waiting for you, offering words of support and encouragement. This is sympathy; they want to help you out of the pit you have found yourself in. This can assist, but not as much as the person who is standing beside you; the person who is in that hole with you and can see the world from your perspective; this is empathy."[1]

There are times when the only thing funeral directors can give is sympathy when it's outside of our ability to fully empathize with a person's situation. After all, the person lying in the casket isn't my father. This isn't my daughter. This isn't my family.

And that's our job. We are paid to be directors. We are paid to be the stable minds in the midst of unstable souls. And honestly, I really can't handle much more. I have learned to maintain a certain level of objectivity because there's only so much pain, grief, and heartache a person can share until I too start to crash and burn. (And boy, have some of us crashed and burned.)

But there are other times when I can't help but be drawn into the narrative. Not just as the director, but as an actual character in the drama of life and death. On this crisp early morning, like everyone else in the room, Pop-Pop and I were drawn into Sara's life. We loaded her into the van and drove back in silence, partially because we were tired and without coffee, and partially because we were taking in everything we had just witnessed.

When we got back to the funeral home, I knew that the family wanted Sara's little body embalmed. I don't like embalming children; I *really* don't like it. I suppose no embalmer enjoys it. The fact that my wife and I are infertile has made me extrasensitive to the sight of dead children.

Fortunately, I had other work to do, so I, somewhat selfishly and somewhat out of self-protection, left my grandfather alone to embalm this young body that had been emaciated by cancer and chemo. He, like me, felt somehow connected to Sara and her family. He's a tactile person and when he's able to give hugs, it opens up his heart, a heart that has found its outflow in practicing a gift he's been perfecting for the past sixty-plus years: embalming.

EMBALMING IS THE SIMPLE process of displacement. We empty the body of its blood while simultaneously filling it with a fluid that stalls and arrests the decomposition process. If you put your finger on the right side of your neck, you can feel the carotid artery pulsating with every heartbeat. That's the artery we open. We incise the neck, then search through the muscle and tendons until we find the carotid artery (and I should add that not all embalmers use the same artery we do). Next to the carotid artery is the jugular vein. We raise both, tying strings around them to keep them separate, and slice a small hole in each. The whole process is kind of like sticking your hand in a bowl of spaghetti topped with tomato sauce and trying to find some penne that's hidden at the bottom.

The embalming machine is a purely pragmatic mechanism. With its Whovian Dalek-like shape, there's no flair or style points to our little Porti-Boy. It has a fluid container on the top, a couple of knobs on the bottom, and when we turn it on, it forces the mixture of embalming fluid mixture through a rubber tube that we connect into the carotid artery. The pressure from the Porti-Boy forces the fluid into the arterial system, pushing the blood out of the jugular vein. It's a pretty thing seeing the crimson red blood flow down our porcelain embalming table. It ebbs and flows in tints and shades like a time-lapse video of the setting sun on a clear fall day.

Even though I have my misgivings about embalming, sometimes embalming provides grieving families a small comfort in a comfortless time. And few embalmers are better at crafting that comfort than my grandfather.

TWO HOURS PASSED AND I stuck my head into the morgue to peek at my grandfather's results. And what I saw was nothing like the girl we had picked up at 6 A.M. Sara's skin, which had a pale grayness to it, was now a healthy-looking flesh tone. Even Sara's size looked more natural, as the embalming fluid filled out some of the weight cancer had taken.

"It's the good Lord!" my grandfather responded when I complimented the embalming job. "He always helps me through the tough ones."

In the solitude of my mind, I doubted that God gave any guiding force to my grandfather's movements. But regardless of whether or not God had helped him, I knew that for my grandfather, the idea that God is present with him in the darkness of this art is exactly what he needs to perform the task of embalming a dead child.

After all, death sits in these tensions of opposites that astoundingly hold us together. In death, we find both the repulsive and the beautiful; perhaps that is nowhere more apparent than in the gruesome, and yet at times beautiful, art of embalming. In death, we find the individual creating community; that perhaps is nowhere more apparent than at a funeral.

The day of the service came. Sara was dressed in a freshly bought dress and laid out in her small, white casket. Flowers from her family flanked either side. My grandfather had worked tirelessly getting the clothes and makeup just right.

And I could tell, by the tired look on his face, that this had pushed him to his physical and emotional limits.

Pop-Pop's gift was such a weird one, so gruesome and barbaric, and yet today, for Sara's parents, Joan and Jim, this was the best they'd seen Sara look for a very long time.

We all have gifts to give during death. These gifts take the form of condolence cards, or a shared story, or a phone call, or food given, or just showing up. The gifts might feel broken. Some of them feel small. Other gifts feel dull. But when all these gifts come together, they form a bigger picture. All these pieces, all these gifts connect during death and create some fuzzy mosaic, some living remembrance of celebration—the best of all possible remembrances—of what the deceased stood for, what and who the deceased loved, and what the deceased meant.

When we walk the earth, we give pieces of ourselves away (and sometimes, like Sara, we give a bunch of Hershey Kisses away). When Sara gave pieces of herself, part of her remained, because the more love you give, the more you live on through your community.

A funeral—however we define "funeral"—is where these parts and broken pieces that you've given away come together and form a communal resurrection of your being, your person in the community of those you've touched. That day, the day of Sara's funeral, we all—including my grandfather and I— came together with our broken pieces. Some of those pieces, like mine, were small and others larger, some dull, some bright. Some pieces were shared stories of Sara's homemade cards. Still others brought chocolate to be placed in the casket. Each piece was a part of the whole. And when all these pieces came together on that day, at that funeral, there, in the center of such grief, was a sense of such joy. Her death, like her life, created something beautiful: us.

After the viewing and funeral, we ushered everyone out of the chapel for the closing of the casket. Sara's parents, as well as her paternal and maternal grandparents, stayed, along with my grandfather and me. The tears started flowing. My grandfather stood—as is his custom—right in the middle of the family, with his arms around the shoulders of those closest to him. Today, his arms were around Sara's father, Jim, and Sara's mother, Joan.

After a minute of staring in silent tears, Joan embraced my grandfather. Laying her head on his shoulder, she began to sob, finally choking out, "Thank you. Thank you. Thank you." Her words were directed at Pop-Pop for all the work he had done to make Sara look so beautiful. But, as much as Sara looked alive in that casket, Sara's life—everything she gave—had brought her back today. We, all of us, were Sara's mosaic and for this time, even though Sara had died, we—Sara's family, friends, and even us funeral directors—had brought her back to life.

12

HEAVEN ON EARTH

I was outside parking cars in a funeral procession line when a hot rod truck, with yellow racing stripes and a flare side bed, pulled up into the procession line. Our funeral home's parking lot is laid out in such a manner that the only people who just "pull up" in the procession line are the ones who have done it before. Although I didn't recognize the truck, as soon as I saw it pull into the procession line without any need of my direction, I was pretty sure I'd recognize the face of the driver, since he or she was probably a regular at the funeral home.

It was Donnie Smith. Donnie stepped out of his truck, and we chewed the fat for about twenty minutes. He told me that his dad, Donnie Sr., had health issues that might be directing him to us in the not-too-distant future.

There are some people I know only through funerals, and Donnie's one of them. We buried his daughter a couple of years back, and because Donnie knows half the people in Chester County, he finds himself at funerals nearly as much as I do. Today he was here for a friend's funeral, and we put him to work as the door tender, greeting everybody who came through the front door with his genuine smile and warm presence.

The next day we conducted four more funerals, which is the maximum amount of funerals our small family-run funeral home can handle. It was a long day that capped a busy month. I was in seminary at the time and was working on a finals essay that was due the following day. The combination of a busy work schedule and finishing up a finals essay pushed me closer to that drained place of compassion fatigue.

Later that evening, after I had gotten home late, my phone rang at around 10 P.M. *Certainly, it can't be a death call,* I thought. *Everyone knows I'm finishing my final tonight.*

"Caleb, we have a death call and I need you to go on it," my grandfather said.

"Can't anyone else go? I'm working on my essay that's due in a couple hours."

"Nobody else is picking up their phone."

My countenance was a walking curse word as I knew this death call would put me right up against my deadline. And my paper was still unfinished. I dreaded the thought of turning in an unfinished product because "nobody else is picking up their phone."

"Who died?" I asked.

"Donnie Smith," Pop-Pop replied.

"Yeah, I was talking to Donnie's son yesterday. He said he knew this was coming, but I don't think he was expecting it this quickly."

"It's not Donnie Senior," Pop-Pop said. "It's Donnie Junior."

I was shocked, angry, and tired but had to quickly move past that and into action. I called a friend to help me out with the removal; we got into the van and we took the twenty-minute drive to Donnie's house. We pulled up to a house packed with all Donnie's family and friends. Donnie had gotten up that morning like normal, eaten his breakfast, then lain back down "because he was feeling tired"—and never woke up. He'd been struggling with some heart issues, so Donnie's doctor was going to sign off in order to keep the coroner's saws out of Donnie's chest.

Walking into these types of unexpected death situations is like walking into another world. The family and friends are all on different schedules. Those who are sitting on the bed of the deceased aren't wondering about dinner, or how they're going to pitch their project at work.

Time has slowed to a pedestrian pace, and they sit in grief, resisting the reality that what was their husband, their wife, their son, daughter, grandfather, friend is no longer present to hug, laugh, and live with. No warning, no time for Donnie's family to say good-bye, no time to tie up loose ends. Just the day before, he told me how he was taking care of his dad. Nobody expected this. He didn't expect it. In life, few things are worse than a loved one leaving without saying good-bye.

Death creates its own culture. Here, language is spoken with fewer words and more tears, hugs, and contemplation. The regular dress code doesn't exist, and the norms and mores of society are put on hold. Here, in this sacred space, God seems nearer; family and friends surround you; you can let your emotional inhibitions go. This is the world that was never meant to be and yet is everything you wish it could be. As I noticed at Chad's funeral, it seems we have to go back through death to get to Eden.

At Donnie's house everybody was crying, holding one another, generally more compassionate than they normally would be. And I was the colonialist, walking into another culture, ready to impose society's desire for a clean picture of death. And, boy, was I ready to colonize this world. I had to get back to finish up my final. I was tired. While they had forgotten time, I was on a strict schedule.

This particular situation, though, was a little over the top. Donnie's daughter was lying in the bed with her deceased father and refused to leave, which set off a chain reaction of emotions and tears. I have had people run after us yelling *Bring back my mama!* as we drove away, but I've never seen someone lie in the bed with their dead father, refusing to leave him. My friend whom I brought with me to help with the removal had never seen anything like this, either. He was standing frozen in the corner like a deer caught in headlights.

The daughter's boyfriend was crying so hard he could barely breathe and had to be held up by some of the family members. He would suck in a gulp of air with one huge breath, then let out a burst of tears for about thirty seconds, only to suck in another breath, thus preventing himself from hyperventilating.

Sometimes, especially when I'm in full-on professional mode and nearing compassion fatigue, I find myself wishing that the bereaved could be more self-controlled with their emotions. And on days like today, after four funerals and a final due in a couple hours, I just didn't have time for this. I used to say that compassion fatigue is like a callus, a spot where you just don't feel things the same way. And while that's true, the callus of compassion fatigue usually covers up a scabbed wound. When you see emotions like this, it makes you fearful and defensive because you're afraid your wound will be opened up again.

After seeing all the tears, my compassion fatigue started to get chatty in my head. I thought to myself, *Come on, guys. Donnie probably wouldn't want you all acting like this. See what love's gotten you into? You're making yourselves look like a bunch of overemotional, sentimental, touchy-feely human beings. You have allowed death to affect you. Death isn't that hard. We all have to deal with it. Maybe you all could approach this with a little more objectivity.*

Quickly realizing my own callousness, I told my brain to quiet down and I tried my best to watch and listen. As I watched with renewed purpose, I saw the tears and the weeping, but I also saw something beautiful. Sometimes positive reframing overlooks the reality of certain situations, but other times, we have to look for the positive if we want to keep moving. As I watched, I saw the tears, but I also saw the hugs. I saw the emotions, but I also saw the deep grief that flowed from deep love. I saw the death, but I also saw the life. By the end of our time there, I was a part of their family. They were hugging me and crying on my shoulder, and I couldn't help but think how right this world was. I felt like I had touched a bit of heaven, and my soul treasured it. Even my friend remarked at how touching the whole thing was for him.

With renewed eyes, I saw a rare moment where heaven was born. I saw a community honestly express the horribleness of death. In a rare moment, I saw how death and dying creates community by allowing us to touch one another's humanity. To be human is not to be closed off, detached, emotionless, and on a strict schedule. Being human means the opposite: connecting, being fluid, feeling, and—at times—weeping. Ironically, sometimes heaven happens when we're closest to hell. Because heaven is wherever love reigns, even in those circumstances that are painful and full of tears. Sometimes heaven even happens on earth.

FOR A LONG TIME, especially as a teenager and young man, heaven, for me, was less about love and more about a means to provide solace from the uncertainty of death. It was, to a degree, an extrinsic religiosity that clothed my frail skin from the coldness of mortality. After hearing a sermon one Sunday that challenged me otherwise, I tried to distance my attachment to heaven, with the hope that I could find a religion that provided more than a self-serving solace from death.

I wanted a spirituality that wouldn't collapse with the removal of heaven.

I wanted a spirituality that made room for the voice of death and the value that death's voice brought to life.

After questioning hell, I then began to cross the Rubicon of religion: I started to not only question my motives for wanting heaven, I also started to question the existence of heaven. When I first started blogging, the idea that a funeral director could put his thoughts into words in a semipopular format was a novelty that attracted some interviews from national news organizations. One journalist in particular was interviewing me for two different publications at once. One publication was a national religious publication, and the other was for a local newspaper's "slice of life"-type column.

The interview took place shortly after Robbie's funeral, a funeral that caused a domino effect for many of my beliefs, including my beliefs in heaven. I shared some of my doubts with the reporter, and I told her that she could write about my heavenly doubts in the religious publication, but not in the local newspaper because I knew that my family and friends would likely see the local newspaper article but wouldn't lay eyes on the religious publication. To my dismay, the newspaper article printed everything I had told the journalist.

I didn't know what to do. I wasn't sure how my doubt disclosure would affect my relationships with my family, my friends, and the business. Would people go to another funeral home because "Caleb doubts heaven"? I was afraid that doubting heaven would put me in "the other" category, and that I'd be slightly ostracized in my strong religious community.

My family was both upset and concerned for my salvation. They interpreted doubt to be the same as disbelief, as though my questioning of the afterlife meant that I was 100 percent certain it didn't exist. My mom questioned whether or not I was still a believer; my aunt cried for my soul; another aunt told her pastor she was upset with me; and I had random people at funerals tell me they were praying for my salvation. One person in particular pulled me aside after a funeral and "laid hands on me" (a forceful prayer technique that's equal parts zeal and awkward).

This was another Holy Saturday experience for me. When

the Christian calendar comes to Good Friday (the day the church remembers Jesus's death), it's easy to skip over Saturday in anticipation of the joyous and triumphant Easter Sunday when Jesus rises from the dead. We've read the end of Jesus's story, giving us the ability to both fast-forward through the painfulness of his death and reinterpret that end into the Saturday immediately before it. The contrast in the story from death to resurrection makes Saturday a pretty boring day, but a little imagination about the unfolding of this three-day narrative makes Saturday the most relatable for me. On Saturday, Jesus's followers had little to no knowledge of what was to come on Sunday. They existed in the doubt and deflation of the death of their Messiah. Holy Saturday was a day when Jesus's followers were wallowing in a death of their hope, the death of a friend, and the death of their vision for the future. This was a day when silence and doubt were their only form of worship. And it's a day that many of us experience for a lifetime.

Believers often seem to interpret death in the light of the resurrection. I should say they overlook Good Friday and Holy Saturday because they know what happens on Easter. But skipping ahead to Easter might be what makes so many believers so unfamiliar with the pain, silence, and doubt of death. If there's one reason why believers use comfort clichés—like "You'll see him again someday," "She's in a better place," "God doesn't give you more than you can handle," "Heaven will wipe away all your tears"—it's because they've only read the resurrection chapter of the story, and they've used that chapter as a shield against the darkness of death and anxiety.

This is the problem as I had begun to see it: we've become so focused on the resurrection that we've never taken *death* to heart. Certainly, the afterlife is powerful; and like most powerful things, it's easily abused. The easiest abuse that arises is that we can pay more attention to the life after than the life here and now. And maybe, if we're always looking up for heaven, we miss the heaven that's right in front of us.

And that's the danger in it all, that we start to value the heaven after life more than we value the heaven here in life. After all, despite what I thought as a young man, the good news isn't about bringing somebody to heaven. It's about heaven coming down to meet us.

In most of our minds, if God exists, God exists in heaven, and—by implication—not on earth, which makes sense in the heaven-centered orientation that assumes heaven is all that is good, and earth is all that is hardship, decay, and eventual death. But in a death positive and earth positive orientation, maybe God dwells here with us too? Maybe God isn't above, but in, through, and with us, making "heaven" possible here. Maybe it can happen simultaneously with death.

THAT DAY WE PICKED up Donnie at his home, the community that I saw there wasn't what we think heaven would look like. There were tears. There was death. There was pain. But there was also deep love. And, if I believe that God dwells with the broken, God was there too.

It was these experiences that allowed me to find heaven again. It wasn't "up there." Nor was it after death. Heaven was happening wherever love was being born. I also used to think heaven is all big, with pearly gates, mansions, and roads paved with gold. But I started to find that it was really present in the small, mundane tokens of kindness and grace. Heaven hides in plain sight.

Probably close to three hundred people came through the church during Donnie's viewing. Before we began the service, we invited the family up front to the casket to say their good-byes. At this point, I usually stand at the foot of the casket and observe what is often one of the harder moments for a bereaved family to handle: the last moment you have to touch, look at, and speak to the deceased. After the family says their good-byes on a day none of them expected to come so soon, we close the lid.

While this family was still having their final moments around the open casket, I noticed something right in front of me. Sitting in the front pew of the church were two little girls—one a blonde, the other a brunette (which is how I'll distinguish them from here on out)—both about seven years old. The brunette was wearing what appeared to be her white Easter dress, her hair combed straight and her shiny white dress shoes fitted to feet that were dangling back and forth off the floor. Next to her the little blond girl was dressed in black pants and a black shirt. I guessed they were Donnie's granddaughters.

As most of the adults were crying, the blonde reached her arm across the back of the brunette and held her, at which point tears started to roll down the brunette's porcelain face. They didn't know I was watching them, and as far as I know, I was the only one looking at them, as all the adults were huddled around the casket.

The blond girl got up, walked back to the second pew, and opened an old Phillies cigar box that she was using as a kind of purse. She opened the lid, reached into the box, pulled out a tissue from the stack she had neatly placed in the box, and rushed back over to where she had been sitting only seconds before, catching the tears as they ran down the grief-filled face of her friend.

At this point I got emotional. There's a certain sense of hardness that creeps in after years in this business. And I'll be the first to admit that few things bother me, few things touch me anymore. Death makes us into altogether different creatures; we can become like rough-skinned rhinos who need something incredibly poignant to pierce our outer shell.

I watched the compassion from this young girl for a couple of minutes and then I saw my grandfather nod in my direction, causing me to switch back to my job at hand, which was the task of closing the lid.

Sometimes the very best we can hope for, the most beautiful of our humanity and a world that is made of love—heaven—happens at a funeral, when a little girl wipes away another little girl's tears.

We have this assumption that heaven and death are total opposites, that one can't dwell with the other like oil and water. But my experience has been different. Because love is born around death, heaven makes its quiet entrance in these small but beautiful moments. Death and heaven are connected in ways we might not be able to see or feel. Death and heaven are like dirt and flower, and when heaven happens here on earth, death is somewhere in the mix allowing heaven's beauty to bleed through into the here and now. Not in spite of death, but sometimes because of death. Today, here on earth, in the midst of death and pain, heaven exists.

13

SAM MCKINNEY'S MYSTICISM

S am McKinney came from an entrenched Parkesburg family. Like my family, her family had lived and died in Parkesburg dirt, becoming a part of it and it of them. Like most families in this area, we've buried generations of McKinneys and they know us and consider us an extension of their family. They know our stories, and we know theirs, and that's the way we like it. We all knew Sam was gay and we all knew that her forty-year-old body was being cruelly invaded by cancer that had started and spread from her lungs.

As a community, Parkesburg had recently started to become more accepting and welcoming of its LGBTQ citizens, affording Sam and her friends the ability to more easily find one another and form a strong and involved public voice in our borough. In Parkesburg and throughout the rest of the country, the mainstream prejudice toward the LGBTQ community is being dispelled and replaced. Where it lingers, however, is within some churches, where long-held beliefs and an unhealthy tribalism still paint the LGBTQ community as "unnatural" and "other." That's why when Sam's parents came into the funeral home to make funeral arrangements, their first request caught us by surprise.

"Sam wanted her funeral in her church."

Because Sam was openly gay, she wasn't allowed to be a member of her family's home church, but she loved God, loved her church family, and found enough motivation to make her way to church once in a while. The fact that she wanted to be a member but couldn't was a fact known by more than a few, which is why the impact of the request knocked down my learned professional cadence. In a rare moment, my mouth became unhinged from my mind, and I blurted out, "Why would Sam want to have her funeral in a church that rejected her?"

Sam's mom looked at me with her fierce eyes, eyes that had no doubt grown fiercer every time she defended her daughter, and she passionately replied, "Sam loved God, and she always wanted God's people to embrace her. What she couldn't have in life, she'll receive in her death."

Sam and her family wanted to rise above the tribalism. It

reminded me of a story I once read about Dorothy Day, who would later become one of the prominent social activists in the twentieth century. When Dorothy was eight years old, she experienced the 1906 San Francisco earthquake that killed over three thousand people and destroyed nearly 80 percent of the city. Her family lived in the neighboring city of Oakland, which soon became a refuge for the displaced survivors from San Francisco. In her autobiography, she writes:

> When the earth settled, our house (in Oakland) was a shambles . . . but there was no fire in Oakland. The flames and cloudbank of smoke could be seen across the bay and all the next day the refugees poured over by ferry and boat. Idora Park and the racetrack made camping grounds for them. All the neighbors joined my mother in serving the homeless. Every stitch of available clothes was given away.[1]

This unreserved generosity and sense of boundless community that she saw during the tragedy had a lasting impact on Day. She continues,

> While the crisis lasted people loved each other. It makes one think of how people could, if they would, care for each other in times of stress, unjudgingly in pity and love.[2]

Like Day, I have seen how death has a way of sweeping us out of our tribalism and prejudice, allowing us to see and appreciate the humanity in everyone, even in those we dislike or disagree with. I saw it most directly at Sam's funeral.

I called the pastor of Sam's church, not sure how she'd respond to the McKinneys' request. Would she embrace Sam's request? Or, would she, in an attempt to defend her tribe, categorize Sam as "other" and politely decline Sam a church funeral?

"Hi, is this Pastor Jackson?" I asked.

"Yes," the pastor replied.

"I'm meeting with the McKinney family," I paused. "I'm sure you're aware that Sam died last night."

Her voice cracked as she said, "Yes."

"In talking with the family, they were wondering if Sam's funeral could—" At that point Pastor Jackson cut me off.

"Be at the church," she finished my sentence and continued, "I've been visiting with Sam these past couple weeks, offering her Communion and encouragement. She told me everything she wanted. Her funeral belongs in her church."

Pastors and funeral directors often share "hearse talk" on the way to a funeral. Based on some past hearse talk Pastor Jackson and I shared, I knew that Sam's pastor wasn't entirely comfortable with the mainstream move toward LGBTQ acceptance, so I was surprised that she had been visiting Sam, let alone would allow Sam's funeral in the church. If there is one thing I have noticed time and again, it's that death and dying has a way of breaking down barriers, allowing us—for a moment—to find common ground in our humanity. It has a way of taking a church that officially excludes the LGBTQ community and enabling them to see the importance of people over opinion. Henri Nouwen writes, "However different we are, we were all born powerless, and we all die powerless, and the little differences we live in between dwindle in the light of this enormous truth."[3] Sam's pastor found that enormous truth that dwindled her opinions she had once thought so important.

What I experienced that day at Sam's funeral was nothing like I had expected. Nothing like I deserved.

Pastor Jackson delivered a beautiful eulogy and message and we all left the building knowing that Sam's funeral had done something special, something deeply human for us all. The sanctuary was a mix of Sam's family (some of whom didn't feel comfortable with Sam's lifestyle), her LBGTQ community, and Sam's church family, many who, though they loved Sam, didn't feel comfortable with her sexuality. But that day, Sam brought us all together in unity and love. And together, the entire group of us brought Sam to her final resting place as a unified whole, united by life, united by death, worshipping as one.

LOOKING BACK, I REALIZE that what I experienced that day at Sam's funeral was an introduction to death spirituality. A spirituality of death shows us how death is the mystical unifier that helps us see the delusions of our tribal divisions and stitches us back together. Death inspires us to empathy, to embrace. It's the common denominator for all humanity that connects us into one, so that when someone outside our tribe dies, we can—if we try—feel the pain and respond, not in fear, but in love.

Some of us, like myself, have experienced this mystical belonging with a sense of the divine; but all of us, from young to old, from rich to poor, from friend to enemy, we all know the mystical belonging of death that tears down borders, as it did between Sam and a closed church. We have to try to find fear in our belly when someone outside our tribe is grieving. We have to pursue our fear to its fullest when we're witnessing the stranger die a grueling death. And this is a major part of what it means to find a death spirituality.

But we don't all find this death spirituality. Sometimes, instead of allowing death the opportunity to inspire our compassion and love, we give into the death negative narrative of fear, bitterness, and isolation. Death can give people the opportunity to cultivate more fear. It makes us build walls. It makes us want to control things so that they're more predictable, more powerless. Death is that thing that makes our brain boil with fear. The terror of it—the fear of it—can make even a good person devolve into something less than human.

Death can either bring
unity or disunity,
love or hate,

peace or war,

healing or pain,

embrace or exclusion,

silence or fundamentalism,

heaven or hell,

mortality positivity or mortality shaming,

a broken-open heart or a broken-apart heart.

And yes, life is often a mixture of both, but somewhere along the way, we must choose if we will embrace fear or resurrection, choose the death negative narrative or be inspired and be filled with the death positive narrative.

The Christian message, the thrust of the church Sam wanted to be a part of, is that death doesn't have to lead us to fear, to hatred of the other, and to sin, but can lead to new life, even a better life, that even in death, we can find a way to "forgive them for they know not what they do," embrace them, and include them, much like Sam and her ability to give her beauty to the church. On the day of Sam's funeral, in a church that saw Sam as the other, Sam brought resurrection into my heart. She was being like Jesus even in death.

With death we can find ourselves. With death we can find the ideal of humanity that Dorothy Day spoke of. With death we can find a community of the broken, coming together to make a whole. With death we can be inspired to a spirituality that is centered around empathy, compassion, and understanding.

This is the tension of who we are: on one hand, we find our deepest suffering and agony in death, and on the other, we find our highest beauty. This liminal state of the between of death is a tension we can resist with the sword and armor of a death negative narrative, or it can be embraced with a better narrative, a narrative of a good death, of a death spirituality.

For me, that day I chose the death positive narrative, and in doing so, my story and my relationship with death had begun to turn, and soon after Sam's funeral, I found myself ready to allow death into my life.

14

ACTIVE REMEMBERING

When Jennifer died, she died suddenly at her home in her sleep without there being an apparent cause of death. Jennifer, who had Down syndrome, was in her late forties and lived with her parents, Kathy and Don, who were in their late seventies and both retired. Don went to wake Jennifer up in the morning and found her lying peacefully in her bed with no apparent signs of a struggle. Jennifer was taken to our county's morgue where the coroner did her work in trying to determine the cause of death.

"Coroner's cases," as we call them, typically involve an autopsy, toxicology tests, and any other examinations that the coroner deems necessary. It usually takes a day for coroners to do their hands-on work, and at that point, they release the body to us, so we can get started on our hands-on work of repairing and restoring all of their hands-on work. The toxicology tests, which involve blood tests and other such things that can't be tested with the naked eye, usually take a couple weeks to be completed by a lab, which means that the final cause of death isn't determined and the final death certificate isn't issued until a couple of weeks after the deceased's demise.

For Jennifer, the final death certificate came in the mail to our funeral home a little over three weeks after her death, and about two weeks after her funeral. I called Jennifer's parents, got a hold of her mother, Kathy, and let her know that we had received the final, that we'd have certified copies by the next morning, and that I'd be willing to run them over to their house as soon as we got them. She agreed and by early afternoon of the following day I jumped in my car, drove a couple of miles to the neighboring city of Coatesville, and rang the doorbell.

I didn't intend to make small talk because there was more work for me to do back at the funeral home, but Kathy insisted that I come into the house, taking me into the living room and offering me a seat. She motioned me to sit on the living room sofa as she opened the nine-by-twelve envelope and pulled out a death certificate and looked it over. "Sudden cardiac arrest due to sleep apnea," she read aloud. "I suppose I should have known. Jennifer's snoring had gotten worse the past couple months." I stopped her before she could continue because I figured she was heading to a place of guilt.

"You loved her so much," I interrupted, "and you took such fantastic care of her." I've used this line on some occasions in similar situations at various times in my funeral directing career, and it usually produces the desired effect of guilt release and tears. Kathy was no different. In between the tears, she started to talk about how lost she felt, how her life had been wrapped around Jennifer's well-being, how her identity had been in loving Jennifer, how she didn't know what to do with all the time she now had on her hands. Her husband, Don, she said, was also having a difficult time finding his bearings in a world without Jennifer.

"Come into the kitchen," she said. I walked through the archway into the kitchen and saw something I'd never seen before. Jennifer's place at the kitchen table was covered with a shrine—a collection of items that had been meaningful to Jennifer. I had associated a shrine with the worship of a demigod or saint, but Jennifer's family took the broader meaning. They dedicated this spot entirely to the memory of their daughter.

"We thought it'd be a good idea," Kathy said. I was slightly taken aback by the whole thing. If you had asked me the first word that came to mind when I saw it, I would have said *weird*, maybe even *pathological*. But after Kathy started to explain the different parts of the shrine and their meanings, I understood my reactions had been hasty.

"The teddy bear was her favorite stuffed animal. Don gave it to her years ago; she got attached to it, and she took it with her wherever she went. I thought about putting it in the casket, but it's a piece of her that I want around. It still smells like her."

Kathy pointed at some drawings. "I had Jennifer's younger nieces and nephews draw icons of Jennifer, so that's what these are." The icons weren't great pieces of artwork, but they had obviously been given great care in their making.

And in the center of the shrine was a professional, framed photo of Jennifer surrounded by some wilted flowers that had likely been pulled from funeral baskets, and some Yankee candles that were halfway burned. Jennifer's baby booties were in the mix as well as a couple of random photos of Jennifer's family and friends. And a jar of sand from the beach at Ocean City, New Jersey, Jennifer's favorite place.

The more Kathy explained the shrine, the more the whole thing became so much more meaningful. After I left Kathy and Don's house, I didn't have a context to explain why Jennifer's shrine meant something to me. It took me a couple of years before I started to make a distinction between closure, passive remembrance, and active remembering. Passive remembrance happens when we stumble upon an old photo of a deceased loved one. It happens when we don't expect it, remembering that is unplanned, sad but beautiful. Active remembering has the same end, but it happens on purpose, when we make a point to remember.

A VERY POPULAR AMERICAN pastor recently wrote in one of his books that grief should only take a "few months." The pastor goes on to say, "You must get beyond it. Unless you let go of the old, God will not bring the new. It is natural to feel sorrow and to grieve, but you shouldn't still be grieving five or ten years later."[1] As much as I disdain this passage of his writing, it's not entirely his idea, since so many of us believe the end of grief work should be closure. Where does this idea that we should "let it go" come from? Why do we, especially Americans, feel the need to "get beyond it" to find closure with our grief and our deaths?

I suppose many of us have the idea that we should find closure because we have a misinterpretation of Elisabeth Kübler-Ross's "Five Stages" model. It's important to know that Kübler-Ross never intended her model to be applied to grief—it was an observation of those going through the dying process. In her work with terminal patients she noticed that the dying would go through stages of denial, anger, bargaining, depression, and acceptance. But before we misinterpreted Kübler-Ross's words, Freud advocated a form of closure called "decathexis," a removal of emotional energy from the deceased, a detachment. Freud suggested that during and after decathexis, we will take those emotional energies and reinvest them into another object or person in a process called "recathexis." His idea, like the misinterpretation of Kübler-Ross's model, is that we find other people to love and use them to fill the "love hole" left by the deceased.

Another reason we are so drawn to this idea of closure is that we like stories that we can control. We like to believe that the lion is tame, that love is never messy, and that death is something we can eventually box up and manage. We like assigning stages to our grief so that it feels more linear, more certain. And we love the idea of timetables so we can predict how long our grief should last, and we can advise our friends, like the pastor, "You shouldn't still be grieving five or ten years later." We want to take all the mystery out of grief, all the messy dirtiness, and all the uncontrolled tears so that it can be neatly wrapped in a hardcover with a beginning and an end. We want to feel like we have power over death. Closure is this perfect sense of how we suppose we should deal with death. But perfection isn't arriving at the end, and it isn't arriving at closure because love lives on after death, and so does grief.

Looking back, I see that my initial problem with Jennifer's shrine was that it didn't portray that strong, American sense of tackling and overcoming grief. Americans love to problem-solve, and we hate sitting in tension, and many of us, even some therapists, see grief as a problem that needs solving, a wound that needs healing, and a chapter that needs closure. But Jennifer's shrine stood in the tension of avoidance and closure and acknowledged that grief is present, it's present in this home, and that is okay. As my friend Father David Hanson told me, icons are windows into heaven. They welcome the deceased back into our lives and allow the deceased to still speak. Instead of giving a timetable to grief and how we relate to the death, an icon or a shrine accepts that grief and death are still here with us even now because we simply have ongoing bonds with the deceased. They will forever be a part of us and instead of trying to "heal" and find decathexis, we must learn to adjust because love has this amazing way of living on past death, in both grief and joy.

You aren't sick with grief; you're healthy with grief.

And you don't need closure; grief will always be the in-between, and that's okay.

In their book, *A General Theory of Love,* Thomas Lewis, Fari Amini, and Richard Lannon write: "In a relationship, one mind revises the other; one heart changes its partner. . . . Who we are and who we become depends, in part, on whom we love."[2] As the authors go on to explain, our neural pathways can quite literally become reflections of who we love, in that our brains have neurologically wired bits and pieces of those closest to us into our minds. Douglas Hofstadter takes this further in his book *I Am a Strange Loop.* He writes, "Every normal adult human soul is housed in many brains at varying degrees of fidelity, and therefore every human consciousness or 'I' lives at once in a collection of different brains, to different extents."[3] In a very real, tangible way, the power of Jennifer's love, the calming effect that she had on her family, this had become a literal part of those she loved and those who loved her. Her inherent goodness had rewired their brains and made them into something better.

Our loved ones don't just affect our neurology; they can also pass down traits of themselves biologically. In Exodus 20, Moses talks about how God visits loving-kindness to a thousand generations of those who are good. This too might be closer to the truth than we can imagine. According to the new insights from behavioral epigenetics (experimental science on how nurture shapes nature), researchers have found that trauma and the psychological effects that come with it can be passed down molecularly from one generation to the next, so that a person's tendency toward depression that was caused by parental neglect, or abuse, and so on is inherited just like physical traits. But love is also passed down from generation to generation. There are literal pieces of your loved ones in you from generations ago. And there will be pieces of your love for generations to come that play out in joy, confidence, and bravery. Love may not be the same as power, and it may not always lead to survival, but love, unlike anything, finds a way to live on.

And this is why the dead are always a part of us. When an individual dies, they're there and not there, both neurologically and even biologically.

This idea of closure is a myth.

If there isn't closure, why don't we simply embrace the presence of the deceased in us? Why don't we engage more actively in our remembrance of those we love? I think the reason why Jennifer's shrine touched me so deeply was because it touched on an incredibly potent death positivity element: it's okay to live with grief. In fact, it might even be healthy.

L'Arche is a community started by philosopher and humanitarian Jean Vanier in 1964 that, in many respects, mimics on a slighter larger scale Kathy, Don, and Jennifer's home in that it houses people with intellectual disabilities with those who assist them. The relationship between the two groups isn't a "client-centered model" where the "professional" takes care of the disabled, but a "community model" where all the residents share life together. One of the more famous L'Arche community members was the late Henri Nouwen, who was a priest, professor at Yale and Harvard, prolific writer, and theologian. While living in L'Arche Daybreak in Ontario for ten years, Henri writes about the death of some of L'Arche's core members:

> We talk about the dead; we have their pictures up. Finally, I realized that Laurie, Helen, and Morris, the three people in the community who died the last few years, are all there. They continue to send their spirit to me. They continue to send their love to me. They continue to tell me what life is about. The more I hold onto their memories, the more it's not just remembering someone who is gone. They are active in my gut,

active in my heart, active in my life. In a way, I realize that I have been given them so that I can live and discover how I live. I need them just as they needed me when they were with me. I continue to need them, and they continue to tell me something about who I am and where I am going and to whom I belong.[4]

This continuing relationship with the dead is a tension that few of us want to acknowledge. A person, we say, is either dead or alive, and anything else is simply too uncomfortable for our binary minds to grasp. But death doesn't bring certainties, it brings silence, and often it brings with it a liminality of being in the in-between, a place that exists where life and death mix, not always in discord, but sometimes in a harmonious ecosystem. These spaces shouldn't be closed off or avoided or reduced to simple outdated spirituality, but embraced through what I like to call "active remembrance," a space where the dead are actively and intentionally remembered.

We see the embracing of this liminal space between death and life in the active remembrance practiced by so many cultures outside the United States, such as the Day of the Dead, Śrāddha of Hinduism, Famadihana in Madagascar, and so many other veneration-of-the-dead practices in different cultures. First world secularization has had many benefits, as we've pushed through magical thinking that often comes with simplistic religion sentiments, but that secularization has also unhinged us from the past and people long gone. Connecting with our dead has so often been surrounded by superstition that we've thrown the dead body out with the bathwater, not realizing that our roots, our spirit, is tied to the past we're afraid to touch. When we say "our dead are still here," it's hard to understand such a statement outside of a religious or perhaps superstitious worldview, but we must find a healthy relationship with our dead in our present space as more than just buried or burned if we're ever to find a healthy relationship with our grief and our experiences with death.

Keeping this relationship with our deceased loved ones, through active remembering, starts with the recognition that there are still windows in our world through which we can see the deceased. The dead still hold spaces all around our lives, and many of these spaces are overlooked. Instead of overlooking these spaces, I say we acknowledge them. When we're sitting down with our extended family for a meal and we've lost one of our members, why shouldn't we speak out the deceased's name and recognize them? It doesn't have to be weird; in fact, if done from the heart, it will feel entirely right. Something simple like, "Before we eat, I'd like to just say that I'm thankful for Grandpa. I miss him and I know he'd be happy we're all together."

I recently received a call from an older gentleman who had lost his wife about a month ago. He wanted to chat and I was willing to listen. He told me that losing his wife was so much harder than he thought it would be. His pastor told him that there was no timetable for his grief and to be patient with his feelings. "I'm throwing nothing of hers out," he told me. "I'm keeping all her stuff right where she put it." He went on to say that every morning he makes her breakfast like he always did when she was alive and that he even bought her a Valentine's gift. "It helps," he finished. "It helps to go through the motions; even though she's not here, I still love her just as much as I did when she was."

NOT EVERYONE KEEPS EVERYTHING of their deceased, and very few of us keep going through the motions, but keeping some of the deceased's possessions and dedicating a space for them is one of those windows that allows us to see the presence of one who has died. The same was true of Jennifer's family and the beautiful shrine to her memory. There's much we can learn from Jennifer's family and the way they keep the memory of their loved one alive and close to them as they move through life.

We all carry the dead with us everywhere we go. They live on in everything we do. Their thoughts are our thoughts. Their love is ours. Even their hurts and pains live on in our bones. It's easy to forget what we don't see. It's easy to think we're entirely independent people who have no attachments, who stand alone in a world we've built all by ourselves. It's easy to allow our memory of our loved ones to only be inspired passively. But it might be easier to actively remember those who have gone before us. It might be easier because it helps us remember whom we've come from, it helps us acknowledge our loss, and it helps us live each moment with the knowledge that we're surrounded by the love of a great cloud of witnesses.

15

FINDING MY WORDS

A couple years ago, when the leaves were falling and yards were decorated with Halloween ornaments, I received an anxious call from a deputy coroner. "Jim Reece has died at his house. All the family is here. He's ready to be taken into your care. Please come quickly," he said with an agitated voice.

The "please come quickly" plea was nearly drowned out by the screaming and wailing coming from the background. I told the coroner that we were running a couple funerals that day and it would take time to free up another person to come with me. "Don't worry about bringing someone else," he told me. "I'll help you. Just come ASAP."

I arrived at the house to find the driveway totally full, the overflow parking streaming out onto the yard. A gathering of about fifteen of Jim's friends and family members were huddled with zombielike stares outside the front door, many with cigarettes in hand. Two cop cars were parked along the side of the road. As is their protocol, the cops are called into these sudden death situations just to make sure there isn't any foul play involved. I put my van in reverse and slowly weaved through the maze of vehicles until I got as close to the front door as possible.

I stuffed a mint in my mouth, checked my tie in the mirror, and put on my funeral director face. The "funeral director face" isn't something I wear all the time. I don't wear it to Walmart or the gym. I don't wear it at home or when I'm with friends because it takes a lot of energy. This face, this persona, is hypersensitive to everything, annoyingly patient, and extremely attentive. I can only wear it for a couple hours before my brain is fried and my body tired. Some funeral directors wear it all the time, but I can't, a fact that still makes me question if I'm made to stay in this profession.

I got out of the van and was quickly greeted by the cops, who told me that Jim Reece had been sick for some time with a nasty combo of heart and liver problems caused by too much alcohol and too much junk food. He was a ticking bomb and nobody really knew how bad he was until today. They led me through the shocked crowd and up to the front door, where I was met by Jim's brother, Carl.

Jim's body lay in the middle of the floor where it had fallen. Around him, at least four people were scream-crying, and another five or six people were staring into nothingness with glazed eyes. Emotions are like yawning; one person starts and it triggers a chain reaction. An older lady was sitting in the recliner chair hyperventilating one minute and yelling the next. The deputy coroner stood in the corner keeping his distance. I'm sure he'd seen numerous tragic deaths, and even though Jim's wasn't a murder or a suicide or a horrific accident, it was obvious that the yelling and crying wasn't something he was used to seeing.

The arrival of the funeral director marks a distinct part in the journey of the body going away from family. When we come through the door, people know what's coming and they often become more distraught. The common thinking is that we should do our job, ignore the emotive environment, and get the body out of the home as soon as possible. But I've found that thinking doesn't work. It only makes people more upset and agitated.

Flashing back to the experience with Donnie's family, I remembered this wasn't my first rodeo in an environment where a sudden death such as Jim's caused deep pain and emotional chaos. This time I was a little wiser about how to handle it. My words would be tempered by my experiences with death and by my experiences with silence. The Reece family needed permission to grieve in their own way and at that moment, they needed me to give them that permission. I had learned they didn't need my platitudes or my religious clichés, they didn't need my strong words of certainty and strength. And they certainly didn't need me coming into the room as the almighty funeral director telling everyone what they should do and how they should all just calm down.

The person who guided me into the home was Jim's brother, Carl. Carl had taken it upon himself to be "the strong one." I could tell he was actively pushing down his own emotions and trying to do the same to everyone else as he announced my entrance. Every time he tried to get his relatives to calm down, it only made things worse. I've seen Carls in other settings and I knew that his way wasn't going to work.

"Carl," I asked, "can you tell me who everyone is here?"

"The three ladies on the floor with Jim . . . two of them are our sisters and that one is his companion," he said with his voice raised over the noise. They were all crying and didn't notice him pointing them out. "This right here"—he pointed to the lady hyperventilating in the chair—"this is our mom."

I wanted to comfort her and thought about what I had recently learned from a hospice nurse about three types of touching: touching with desire, touching with demand, and—the most rare option—touching with devotion.[1] Touching with devotion is an ardent recognition of the value of people . . . it's not forceful or uncomfortable; rather, it's respectful and produces ease. In nearly every life context, these three types of touching are hard to differentiate. If someone randomly touches you at the grocery store, it's not always easy to read if it's desire, demand, or devotion. Even in relationships with those close to us, like our significant others, we can't always immediately tell if their touch is desire, demand, or devotion. But there's one place where the humanizing, respectful, and relaxing touch of devotion is nearly undiluted by desire and demand. That place is death, which is why it is so easy to hug and touch around death and dying.

Jim's mother was sitting in her recliner uncomforted and unaccompanied by anyone else in the room, so I got down on my knees and asked, "Can I give you a hug?" She nodded and returned my embrace with her own. For what felt like a couple minutes, we held each other. At first, her cries grew louder, but soon they started to quiet. And then I started to ask her questions. I didn't pull out any "It's all gonna be okay" or "It will get better" platitudes because I knew they were a lie, more in service of the giver than the receiver. I didn't give in to my own discomfort by spouting off clichés that made *me* feel comfortable. I didn't tell her that I was on a schedule or that she had to "get control of her emotions."

I had come to realize that clichés were my own personal defense mechanisms. They protected my own fears, my own blind happiness, and my own ego at the expense of healthy grief. Prescriptive phrases like the following kept the silence and the discomfort of death at a distance:

"Time will heal your wounds."

"You can get through this."

"You'll see him again someday."

Instead of using these phrases, I have learned to say things that acknowledge the pain in someone else, that give them permission to feel everything their heart is feeling:

"Don't worry about me, take all the time you need."

"It's okay to cry."

"This must be impossibly difficult and I'm so sorry."

Jim's mother and I soon started talking about Jim. She was telling me about how they knew he was sick, but not this sick. How he kept his ailments to himself and never asked anyone for help.

She then addressed the elephant in the room and said, "I don't want you to take him." I told her I'd be happy to stay as long as she wanted me to stay. If she needed a couple hours, that was okay. I purposely said it loud enough so that others in the room could hear it too, because I wanted them to know that there was space and time for all their feelings. I did not want to crowd them or push them to move on. This was their time. Grief is wild. When you try to force it to do anything, you end up killing it. It's like a great white shark—put it in captivity and it dies.

Some time passed, and everyone started talking to one another. Eventually they told me that they were ready. I asked them to help me lift Jim's body onto the stretcher and we all walked out to my removal van.

We loaded him into the van. I closed the back gate and we agreed to a time for the family to come into the funeral home the next morning to finalize the arrangements. They told me they wanted a direct cremation and that they'd like to see Jim again when they arrived. I gave most of them a parting hug and drove back to Parkesburg.

On the way home, I realized that I had begun to find words for death, but they weren't the kind of words I was expecting. For the first time in a long time, I felt like I was ready to start writing again. Writing has always been the way I process life. It's been more of a necessary outlet than a creative craft mainly because I'm not a very good talker. I stumble through my sentences like an offbeat drunk meandering down a sidewalk after he has left the bar. Writing has always felt more natural. I kept a journal through middle school and wrote tirelessly about God in high school and through college. But it had taken me a while to find the words for death. For so long I had filled the silence of death with clichés, religious platitudes, and the solemnity one would expect from a funeral director. I needed time to rest in the silence and let it speak to me.

The words we say after the silence aren't the same words we used before the silence. They aren't prescriptive words about how "everything will be better with time." Nor are they religious platitudes about "how God has a plan." No, these words are brave words that come from the inside and flow outward. These words are naked, vulnerable words that aren't looking for certainty. These words are looking for community. These words are meant to embrace, connect, heal, and even laugh.

The next morning, my wife, Nicki, and I were prepping for our first Halloween with our eight-month-old son, Jeremiah, our only child. He had a couple hand-me-down outfits and we couldn't decide which one he should wear. "Go to work," Nicki said, "and I'll bring Jeremiah over to the funeral home in the outfit we pick." I jumped in my car, drove a couple blocks away to the funeral home, and opened the funeral home's front door with my worn but still functioning key. I didn't hear the alarm alerting me that it needed to be turned off, so I knew I wasn't the first one in this morning. I'm rarely the first one in. Pop-Pop and Dad always beat me.

I went back into the morgue, gloved my hands, and started to set Jim's facial features. I retrieved some eye caps out of the drawer, placed them under his eyelids and closed the lids at the "line of closure." The eye caps' jagged surfaces did their job of keeping the lids shut, so I bypassed the glue that I'd use if they were slightly cantankerous. His mouth was still wide open from the day before. I took a needle and thread under the upper lip, through the left nostril, over to the right nostril, back down to the mouth, and through the lower gums. I tied the two ends of the thread together and the finished product looked like every publicly viewed dead person you've seen. "You look good, Jim," I said as I took my gloves off.

A couple hours later, the Reeces came through the front

door of the funeral home. I sat all ten of them down in our arranging area and introduced them to my dad, who was going to be making the arrangements with them.

My cell phone started ringing soon after. I went back to another room and answered it. It was Nicki. "Can we come to the funeral home and show Pop-Pop Jeremiah's Halloween outfit?" My dad, or "Pop" as Jeremiah came to call him later on, has a Three Stooges type of slapstick humor that hasn't been wasted on Jeremiah, who—at just a couple months old—was belly laughing to Pop knocking a Humpty Dumpty doll off the kitchen table. That shared sense of humor is still strong today as they remain the best of buds. And it's always a breath of fresh air for Pop when Jeremiah stops by the funeral home.

I thought to myself, *Well, the family is here. And Pop is meeting with the family, but why not? Pop could use a Jeremiah-inspired smile or two.*

"Sure," I said. "Bring Jeremiah over."

Bringing an eight-month-old into a funeral arrangement may seem slightly irreverent, but I've learned there's a marked difference between the sacred and the reverent. Sacred moments often happen outside of the smug contexts. They happen in smiles, laughter, mistakes, and sometimes they can happen when an eight-month-old interrupts the funeral making of ten grieving souls. Sacredness isn't this stuffy solemnity that we see so often at funerals. Something is sacred when it allows us to find a deep connection with one another.

John Cleese describes this sacredness when he said "the two most beautiful memorial services that I've ever attended both had a lot of humor, and it somehow freed us all and made the services inspiring and cathartic."[2] Studies done on the subject have helped prove what John Cleese has experienced. They've shown that lightheartedness disengages the fight-or-flight adrenaline surge, allowing us to switch back to some degree of rationality and communal connection. Christopher R. Long and Dara Greenwood conducted a study that showed that as mortality reminders (prompts that make study participants think about death) increased, so did individuals' abilities to find and create humor, helping to relieve them of their death anxiety.[3] It's as though evolution has enabled us to relieve anxiety and the fight-or-flight adrenaline surge through a colorful mechanism. Lightheartedness isn't something for the weak minded; it's very much the opposite. It's an integral part of everything sacred, including the sacredness that comes with death.

A couple minutes later Jeremiah came through the front door wearing his dinosaur costume. The costume was a fluffy onesie that zipped over his whole body, including his head, with just enough room for his chubby little face to peek out. It was a stegosaurus with cute little spikes lined from his tail to his forehead. And all of a sudden, Jeremiah was the center of attention as he crawled around the funeral home with his dinosaur tail wagging behind him. He made his way over to Pop and stopped in front of Jim's mom. He smiled at her, she smiled back, and her eyes started to tear up. He played the part as much as an eight-month-old can do, showing off for his buddy Pop. They all laughed. Jeremiah laughed.

Soon the conversation switched from Jeremiah to Jim as they recalled some of his Halloween costumes. Jim's mother made the costumes herself. She remembered how his first one was a fire-man costume she threw together. She remembered how the first time he wore the costume he ran around the house shooting water out of his mouth "like a fire truck." She wasn't very happy at the time, but today the memory brought her joy. The family members' eyes welled up with tears and their bellies filled with laughter as they recalled the good times they had as kids.

After a couple minutes of bringing Jim back to life, Jim's mother looked at my dad and said, "I think we're ready." He ushered them back to see their Jim one last time before I took him to the crematory. I could tell their hearts were full of mem-ories, of life, and the words they spoke gave them strength to say their last good-bye. This was a sacred moment. They kept talking and laughing as they walked, a completely different at-mosphere from the raw grieving I experienced in their home the previous day, but one that was equally as important for them. This wasn't a solemn walk, bereft of life. The day before, they were in the depths of despair (a sacred moment nonethe-less), but today they found some words and they found some peace—thanks to an eight-month-old clad in a stegosaurus costume—that allowed for a sense of the sacred.

AFTER A COUPLE YEARS of listening and watching in the silence as I performed my duties, I too had gone from the depths of despair to finding some peace. As I began to find my words, I did what nearly every scribovert did at that time . . . I started a blog, which I called *Confessions of a Funeral Director,* a nod to both the spiritual confessions and the honest reflections I incorporated in my blogging. It took me a while to hone my voice, but the way I dealt with Jim's family provided a template: stay away from prescriptive talk, encourage people to remember their loved ones, and use the sacred art of lightheartedness, all for the purpose of creating a space that allowed for death talk and community.

As I was processing my experiences through my blog, it helped me look for good stories that were shareable, sacred, and uplifting. Writing about death helped me find the beautiful aspects of death. I was also starting to find that I wasn't the only one who saw the beauty in death and wanted to talk about it. There are many of us. Many who have found words for the odd goodness of death. And we've come together, connected by our silence, connected by our sacred moments, and connected by our bravery. We've come together to share in our words of brokenness. None of us have found all our words in the face of death, and I can't suppose any of us feel like we've even found the right words, but we've found enough to find one another.

16

YIN AND YANG

Birth and death are often inextricably linked. For me, working around death was just a part of life, but when it came to trying to have a child, my wife, Nicki, and I struggled. Through the long and arduous path, we discovered a biological problem stood in the way of what our hearts wanted. During what became a yearlong process, Nicki and I connected with an adoption social worker I had met at a funeral, went through the home study, background checks, and prying personal questions until, in the early winter months of 2012, we found ourselves ready to be picked by a birth mother.

Around the same time, a young and alone woman named

Julia decided that her life situation wasn't the best for the child growing inside her womb, so she linked up with our adoption agency, chose us as her child's adoptive parents, met us a couple of times, and together we chose the name Jeremiah Michael Wilde a few months before he arrived. She also told us she wanted us at the hospital when Jeremiah decided it was time to make his entrance into the world, a birthday invitation we didn't want to miss.

I was standing at a graveside service, listening to the pastor rest body and mind when I got the call. "Caleb," Nicki said, "Julia's water broke, and she's heading to the hospital. Come home quick." Dad was with me at the graveside service, so I moved ninja-like over to him, whispered what was happening, and jumped in our flower wagon, scurrying back to Parkesburg to pick up Nicki and change into something less formal and funeral-like. After all, I was headed to a birthday. We arrived at the hospital and were welcomed into Julia's room. I made a McDonald's trip for Julia and Julia's mother, and as soon as I got back, we learned Julia was dilated nine and a half centimeters (I eventually ate Julia's french fries a couple of hours later). We stepped out of the room, and after twenty minutes flew by, Jeremiah had entered our world.

We stayed at the hospital for the next couple days, forging a relationship with Julia that remains open and strong to this day. On the day of her discharge from the hospital, we gathered in the prayer chapel for an adoption agency–led adoption ceremony, where tears were mixed with the entire spectrum of human emotions. We were to take Jeremiah home with us after the ceremony was over. Julia held Jeremiah at the beginning of the ceremony, signifying this child was hers. At the appropriate time in the adoption ceremony, Julia handed Jeremiah over to Nicki. Even as I write this I still don't know how Julia did it. After she had given Jeremiah to us, I bent down to hug her, and we embraced for a minute. I don't cry often. In fact, the adoption ceremony may have been the last time I let everything loose.

After the hug, I read a short blurb out loud to Julia that I had written a couple of hours earlier at around 2 A.M.:

We love you. We love you for your strength, we love you for the life you have carried these past nine months, and we love you for giving us the greatest gift anyone has ever given us. The gift we couldn't give ourselves. You have made us whole. You have made us a family with your gift of Jeremiah Michael. We want you to know we will always love you. We will always honor you and we will always respect you. And we will show that honor and love and respect by loving your son with everything we are and everything we have. Rest assured that we will be the best parents we know how to be. We will love Jeremiah with all our hearts. We will be there for him no matter what. We will raise him to be a man of honor and good character. We will raise him to have the utmost respect for the woman who gave him life and carried him in her womb. We promise you we will always hold you in the highest regard, and we will teach Jeremiah to do the same.

As soon as I was done reading the most emotive thing I've ever written, a big glob of cry snot dripped from my nose onto Julia's flip-flop-clad foot. I grabbed a tissue, wiped it off, and—like so many times at funerals—the room went from tears to laughter at the drop of a snot. And like death, adoption is full of these spaces that are equal parts sorrow and joy, simultaneous letting go and embracing; it is a miracle of giving and receiving—a yin and yang of life and new birth, of grief and death. Most of us focus on the new life, the yin part of adoption, where a couple like us opens home and heart to a child that's not biologically their own. Most of us see all the good in that space while overlooking the pain and emptiness the birth mother (and birth father, when present) feel as they give their child into the care of another. This process was not just joy and new life; adoption is death and birth all wrapped up into something brokenly beautiful.

But there we were, the grateful parents of this newborn child, Jeremiah Michael. A perfect child, born in the milieu of imperfection.

PART OF THE SIGNIFICANCE of the whole experience of adopting Jeremiah was that a couple of years earlier I had lost hope in having children because death had crushed both my belief that I could be a good father and my desire for children. Nicki and I got married at a young age. We both wanted kids, but I was in funeral school, and we wanted to wait until I was done. After I graduated and started to work for the funeral home, I was unexpectedly consumed by the death negative narrative, and I knew that as much as I wanted children I was neither ready nor I confident that bringing children into the world was best for them.

I knew that the rhythm of my work schedule, the fragility of my psyche, and my wrestling with death wouldn't combine to make a healthy father. The greatest gift my dad ever gave me was his time. Now, as a funeral director, I realize how hard it was for him to make time for me. He could have worked harder, made more money, and given me cooler things—a better car than an AMC Pacer, and so on—but instead of giving me more stuff, he worked less, made less money, and gave me himself. For much of my marriage with Nicki, I knew I couldn't be like my father because I didn't have much of myself to give.

Compounding the fact that I knew I wasn't ready to be a good dad were the trauma and brain fear from seeing too many lost children. I was afraid. I was afraid we'd lose a child, born or unborn, carried or miscarried, and I didn't know if I could take my professional occupation and mix it with a personal loss.

Erin's story was one such story that stuck out in my mind. Early on in my career, we had served Erin in the burial of her two-week-old son, David. He lived and died in a NICU. When I first met Erin, she was a bereaved young mother who had little family support (the bio dad had left her) and even less financial means.

About a year later she called us to inform us that she had just lost another in the second trimester, only this time it was a daughter they named Molly. It's rare that funeral directors have any involvement with a miscarried fetus, as the size and development make our help superfluous. But Erin, along with Reece—her boyfriend and Molly's father—wanted Molly buried next to David and they wanted us to help.

Two children lost in the span of about two years. With the first child, we gave all our services for free (as we usually do), and we offered our services pro bono again for Erin's second departed child out of respect for her and Reece and the grief they were suffering.

For baby David, we asked the cemetery if they would waive the grave opening cost because Erin didn't have much money. The cemetery is owned by a church located in a neighboring town, and they had done so somewhat begrudgingly the first time for David but for Molly they fought us over the fee that, all things considered, was rather minimal for them, but large for Erin and Reece. After we asked the elder board to waive the fee, they told us, "We may waive some of the cost for this couple, but tell the couple not to do this again!" I hate it when big things step on little things. I was upset at this cemetery, and my heart went out to Erin, whose grief and loss seemed to go unrecognized by this local church.

The loss of a child is hard enough, but there are types of grief in our society that—for one reason or another—aren't recognized, such as the grief over the loss of a pet or perhaps the grief caused by stigmatized suicide or the grief of a birth mother giving away her child. This kind of grief—the kind that is overlooked and unrecognized by society—is called "disenfranchised grief."

Perhaps there's no more common form of disenfranchised grief than that from miscarriages, like Erin's.

Miscarriages cause a silent grief. A nameless grief.

A grief for one who had no connections in life. No schoolmates, no friends, no coworkers, all of which translates to no funeral. A grief that can't be shared. A grief to be borne solely by the ones who conceived. A grief that is carried by the one who may now feel guilt upon silent grief because she miscarried. A grief for hope lost. This is a grief that is often carried alone. A grief that is private and difficult to share. A grief for a nameless soul.

It's often traumatic.

Often bloody. Painful.

Often lonely. Powerless.

I've seen some women (and some men) try to be strong after a miscarriage only to find the grief manifest itself over the next couple months and even years. It's not to be brushed aside. It needs to be validated by family and friends and not downplayed with phrases like, "You'll get over it" or "You can always try again."

At the time, I was in a college religion course for working adults. The professor—who was younger than many of his students—had developed a particularly transparent relationship with us and expressed the need for prayer because his wife had just miscarried. Despite the fact he was asking for prayer, his request was quite smug and short as if it wasn't a big deal. Some of the women in the class quickly asked, "How's your wife doing?"

He responded, "Oh, she's fine. It's just a miscarriage."

To that, another lady quickly rebutted, "It might not be a big deal to you, but it is to her. And if you have that attitude, it will be a bigger deal in months to come." She was right. Months later the professor shared with the class that his wife was suffering from depression and was entering counseling.

Although the trimester of the miscarriage can be a factor in the severity of grief, sometimes—depending on how much hope is invested in the pregnancy—the trimester doesn't matter.

The disenfranchised grief of miscarriages is real. People are just unwilling to validate the grief of a miscarriage, which is probably why, to this day, the cemetery has yet to waive the fee for Erin. They just didn't see it as that big of a deal to warrant their kindness.

But this time, Erin had someone to walk with her through

her grief—Reece. From the time they walked through the funeral home's front door, it was evident that Reece was not only a good man, but he was good to Erin. Even though he too was grieving and suffering from the loss, he managed to place Erin and her needs above his own. Even though Erin's first child—David—wasn't his, Reece was entirely respectful of Erin's wishes to have Molly buried next to David. I don't know if the loss of Molly was bringing them closer together, but it was allowing Reece to show his affection to Erin.

A couple of years after Molly was buried with David, I was working a viewing at a local church, and standing at the register book podium, instructing people to sign and take a memorial card and making small talk about the weather, when Erin walked through the door.

After all these years Erin's story had stuck with me. Partially because I felt like the cemetery had screwed her over, partially because I was struck by how Reece loved her, but mainly because her story had made an imprint on my heart.

"How are you doing?" I asked Erin. A question that was both superficial and probing at the same time. And just as I asked, Reece came through the church door with a loaded car seat carrier and a little toddler trailing him.

"You remember Reece?" Erin asked.

"Of course, I do."

"Well, we're married now!"

"Congrats," I said happily. "And who are these little guys?"

"The youngest is six months, and her name is Aida, and the older one is two, and her name is Jasmine."

I squatted down to Jasmine with tears squeezing out of my eyes. I felt like I was looking at something sacred, something holy as these little ones represent something deep and beautiful in humanity.

Jasmine was a petite thing with big eyes and a bashful smile. "I'm glad to meet you," I said as I shook her hand all professional-like.

I stood back up and quickly wiped the small tears from the corners of my eyes before anyone could see them. As I've already mentioned, I don't cry often. Years of repression for professional purposes have calloused that part of me, but every once in a long while something touches a deep part of me that hasn't been hardened, allowing me this wonderful opportunity to feel again. I knew what seeing Jasmine had touched in me. I had been feeling it for a couple of months. The part of me that wanted children, that believed in myself as a father, that deep desire for life was being exposed. The small little yang in the yin of my consuming death negative narrative had begun to shine through the overlay of shadow.

I felt safe enough to know that I could bring a child into the world, and even though that child would experience suffering, loss, and death, I believed that a mortal world was good enough, beautiful enough, and wonderful enough to make the whole thing worth it.

Soon after meeting Jasmine and Aida, Nicki and I started to try, and by trying I mean having copious amounts of unprotected intercourse. A year passed. No luck. We made an appointment with a fertility specialist, who started pumping Nicki full of hormones hoping that something would eventually take. Cysts ended up taking. Ovarian cysts that required two separate surgeries. Our insurance didn't cover any of the fertility treatments, and as we explored the different options post–hormone treatment, we soon found our bank accounts dwindling along with our hope.

People would often ask us, "When are you having children?" At first, we'd joke our way through that question with an "Oh, we're just practicing right now." But eventually, the question became old, and our answer became more certain: "We won't be having biological children."

We never had a miscarriage or a stillbirth, but I felt like I understood a piece of what it feels like to have hope dashed when we were confronted with the disenfranchised grief of infertility, a grief few understood. It was the backdrop of infertility that made Jeremiah that much more beautiful.

SOMETIMES WHEN WE'RE STUCK in the yin, we can whisper the yang into growing, like the way Reece's love for Erin and recognition of her grief seemed to stoke the embers of their love. We can find the embers of life and blow them into light. It takes care, but we can find life in even the darkest places. Life wants to break through. It wants to shine. It finds ways in the deepest, darkest parts of the ocean, it breaks through concrete and asphalt, it grows in the womb of bodies that have miscarried, and it can even find its way to couples who can't make their own. Life is resilient and brave, and it doesn't believe in "can't" and "won't" and "no." In the midst of the no of death, life says yes, and when we find that yes we can help it breathe, help its embers, and swaddle it in our arms.

But it's not yin *or* yang. It's not death *or* life. It's not a binary of one thing or the other. As much as we've been overexposed to the death negative narrative and underexposed to death positivity, the two narratives aren't enemies; they coexist together as a whole. Death is incredibly difficult. Death brings some of our darkest moments and some of the most seemingly insurmountable trials we can imagine. And death opens up the newness of life.

Death is everywhere, present in every aspect of life. Everything we eat, from greens to meat, in all its wonderful pleasure and presentation, is a sacrifice of nature for our survival. And our bodies, which feed on those greens and meats, if buried, will one day become the food for other creatures, small as they may be. Nearly everything we eat is made up of the dead of something else. In every death is life, a birth of something new. It's usually small life, but it's there, somewhere. Just as Julia's birth and giving away of Jeremiah was a grief and shadow for her, in that act of giving—and death can be an act of giving—she gave us life.

This meshing of these two narratives, life and death, is what makes us. It's inviting death into our life and letting them teach each other. Our mortality—the tension of death and life, our struggle for food, for love, for belonging, for commitment, for life, for shelter—this is the womb of the human spirit. And it's out of the human spirit that we create the spectrum of beauty that the world so needs. The human spirit is what allowed Erin to seek life in the midst of death. The human spirit and the struggle for life is what brought Jeremiah, Julia, Nicki, and me together. Mortality can make us beautiful. It's the embracing of this whole, of the light and dark, day and night that keeps us going in the face of difficulty. Elisabeth Kübler-Ross writes:

> The most beautiful people we have known are those who have known defeat, known suffering, known struggle, known loss, and have found their way out of the depths. These persons have an appreciation, a sensitivity, and an understanding of life that fills them with compassion, gentleness, and a deep loving concern. Beautiful people do not just happen.[1]

Beautiful people can happen in the struggle.

Stephen Colbert, whom most of us know as a pundit, humorist, and late-night host, knows the yin and yang, how death and life dwell together in goodness. When Colbert was ten, he lost his father and two brothers, Peter and Paul, in a plane crash. In Joel Lovell's *GQ* article about Colbert, Lovell writes,

> He was tracing an arc on the table with his fingers and speaking with such deliberation and care. "I was left alone a lot after Dad and the boys died. . . . And it was just Mom and me for a long time," he said. "And by her example am I not bitter. By her example. She was not. Broken, yes. Bitter, no." Maybe, he said, she had to be that for him. . . .
>
> "It was a very healthy reciprocal acceptance of suffering," he said. "Which does not mean being defeated by suffering. Acceptance is not defeat. Acceptance is just awareness." He smiled in anticipation of the callback: "You gotta learn to love the bomb," he said.

This phrase "you gotta learn to love the bomb" is a reference to Colbert's time in improv comedy, a form of comedy that has a high degree of potential failure. Colbert then refers to the "bomb" again when he retraces his story back to the death of his father and two brothers:

> "Boy, did I have a bomb when I was 10. That was quite an explosion. And I learned to love it. So that's why. Maybe, I don't know. That might be why you don't

see me as someone angry and working out my demons onstage. It's that I love the thing that I most wish had not happened."[2]

Seeing the whole is hard. We want to see just the black or the white of something. The right or the wrong. We love binaries like Democrat or Republican, Male or Female, Night or Day, Life or Death, Love or Hate. Binaries help us move about a complex world, but they aren't always helpful because it's sometimes an "or" but it's mostly an "and." We, like Colbert, can come to love the thing we hate.

Death, when we embrace it, can be a wellspring of life.

JEREMIAH IS NOW FOUR years old. The mixture of death and life has affected me as a parent. Sometimes I hover for fear that the worst-case scenario will somehow occur. And sometimes (okay, most of the time) I find myself anxious about his safety. I've bought cars that are outside my budget because they score high safety ratings. I double- and triple-check on him at night, softly placing my hand on his chest just to make sure he's still breathing.

But my closeness to death, our struggle with infertility, and Julia's love and bravery for Jeremiah have also allowed me to deeply value his life. I'm so thankful—I mean this in all sincerity—for every moment we spend together, every wrestling match, every book read, every meal shared, every question, every teachable moment, and even the tough times, the bad attitudes (mine and his), the tantrums, and the times he takes wrestling a little too far. Recognizing how short life can be helps me be present, it helps me when I'm tired, it helps me when I'm grumpy and lacking in patience. I'm by no means the ideal parent, but death and my awareness of it have helped me be better. I don't think I'd be nearly as grateful, nearly as patient, nearly as present, and nearly as in love with Jeremiah if it wasn't for my full knowledge of the struggle and brevity of life.

In many ways, I owe much of my goodness to death.

TEN CONFESSIONS

An Epilogue

Over a decade ago I reluctantly joined my family's business. The business of death. Daily I am around grief, heartbreak, tears, snot, and other less-than-charming bodily fluids. I am often the first called to a home, the last at the funeral service or graveside, called first thing in the morning and late at night.

In some ways, I didn't choose this, and in other ways, I'm glad I landed here because I've found a spirituality that I never thought possible. I've found a spirituality that's not only a part of my profession, but also hits at the core of who we are as humans. We are mortal. And instead of being fearful of our mortality and our eventual death, I believe that both mortality and death can enliven us to become more true to ourselves, and those around us.

Over time working this unusual job, I've come to learn and believe ten things about the spirituality of death, and those are the ten things I want to leave you with. Let it guide you to embracing a more positive understanding of death, a life filled not with fear, but with reverence for what we gain when we lean into it.

1. The death negative narrative says there is nothing good in death. This narrative is our evolutionary heritage, and it's been normalized through the news cycle and perpetuated by the way we have hidden death and dying in medical facilities and professionalized death care in funeral homes. This narrative does not tell the whole story. Death is a normal part of life, and when we come to a healthy understanding of it, beauty is found. **Let death show you goodness.**

2. Death cannot be tamed. Death can either break us open or it can break us apart. Those who are broken open find more room for compassion, understanding, forgiveness, and the Other. **Let death break you open.**

3. Death cannot be ignored or rushed past. Death opens up a unique space, giving us time to pause and reflect

on our life's meaning. **Let death make you pause, take a death Sabbath, and reflect, meditate, and take inventory of your life.**

4. Focusing on heaven or the afterlife can cause us to downplay and ignore the value of earth, and of death. Learning to live in the here and now helps us find the goodness of earth, even the goodness in death. **Let death show you what is good about your life here and now, and appreciate that.**

5. The voice of death is silence. The more we can embrace the silence, the more we can embrace death. **Let us embrace silence, rather than trying to needlessly fill it.**

6. The death negative narrative shames our mortality. A death positive narrative invites us to find our true selves in our mortality. **Let it invite us to be more patient with others and ourselves as we learn, grow, and overcome.**

7. Sometimes, our experiences during periods of death and dying are the closest we get to heaven on earth. The community that death creates holds remnants of Eden. **Let us lean into this community and appreciate our relationships in these times.**

8. Death is the great universal that allows us to find the humanity in others, giving us the opportunity to come together despite our differences. **Let us, in death, find love for those we may otherwise dislike.**

9. Active remembering acknowledges that there is no such thing as closure and invites the dead back into our lives. **Let us practice active remembering, acknowledging that the dead never truly leave those they loved.**

10. Embracing death is the key ingredient for a life well lived. **Let us embrace death, realizing that the closer we become to our mortality, the more we confront death, the more we can embrace life.**

ACKNOWLEDGMENTS

I'd like to thank Dad and Pop-Pop for not firing me when this project stole time away from work. And I'd like to thank Nicki and Jeremiah for providing me with ample amounts of love and coffee to fuel me through my numerous episodes of writer's block. Finally, I'd like to thank the community of Parkesburg for letting me see your beautiful souls in all their vulnerability and depth.

NOTES

CHAPTER 1: DEATH NEGATIVE

1. The illustrious Caitlin Doughty coined the term "death positive."

CHAPTER 3: BROKEN OPEN

1. Nicholas Wolterstorff, *Lament for a Son* (Eerdmans, 1987), p. 90.
2. This distinction between the broken-open heart and the broken-apart heart comes from Parker Palmer's article, "The Broken-Open Heart," *Weavings: A Journal of the Christian Spiritual Life* 24, no. 2 (2009).
3. Many believe this quote to be attributed to Ian Maclaren.

CHAPTER 4: DEATH SABBATH

1. Lauren Winner, *Mudhouse Sabbath* (Paraclete Press, 2003), p. 29.

CHAPTER 6: SACRED DUST

1. Krista Tippett, *Becoming Wise* (Penguin Press, 2016), p. 25.

CHAPTER 8: FRONT-DOOR POLICY

1. Elisabeth Kübler-Ross, *Death: The Final Stage of Growth* (Scribner, 1997), p. 5.

NOTES

CHAPTER 9: LISTENING TO THE VOICE OF SILENCE

1. David Rock, "SCARF: A Brain-Based Model for Collaborating with Others," *NeuroLeadership Journal* 1:4.

CHAPTER 11: SARA'S MOSAIC

1. See https://healthpsychologyconsultancy.wordpress.com/2011/08/11/empathy-versus-sympathy/.

CHAPTER 13: SAM MCKINNEY'S MYSTICISM

1. Dorothy Day, *The Long Loneliness* (HarperOne, 2009), p. 22.
2. Dorothy Day, "The Long Way Home" section in Robert Ellsberg, ed., *Selected Writings* (Orbis, 2005), p. 11.
3. Henri Nouwen, *Our Greatest Gift* (HarperCollins, 1994), p. 26.

CHAPTER 14: ACTIVE REMEMBERING

1. Joel Osteen, *Your Best Life Now* (New York: FaithWords, 2004): 146.
2. Thomas Lewis, Fari Amini, and Richard Lannon, *A General Theory of Love* (Vintage, 2001), pp. 143–44.
3. Douglas Hofstadter, *I Am a Strange Loop* (Basic Books, 2007), p. 258.
4. Michelle O'Rourke, *Befriending Death: Henri Nouwen and a Spirituality of Dying* (Orbis, 2009), quoted on p. 95.

CHAPTER 15: FINDING MY WORDS

1. Marie de Hennezel, *Intimate Death* (Alfred A. Knopf, 1997), p. 50.
2. "John Cleese on Creativity," YouTube video, 36:09, from a 1991 lecture on creativity in management to Video Arts, posted by "Johnny V," April 15, 2015, https://youtu.be/9EMj_CFPHYc?t=24m24s.

3. Christopher Long and Dara N. Greenwood. "Joking in the Face of Death: A Terror Management Approach to Humor Production," *International Journal of Humor Research,* 2013 DOI: 10.15

CHAPTER 16: YIN AND YANG

1. Kübler-Ross, *Death: The Final Stage of Growth,* p. 93.
2. Joel Lovell, "The Late, Great Stephen Colbert," *GQ Magazine,* August 17, 2015.

DISCUSSION QUESTIONS

CHAPTER 1: DEATH NEGATIVE

1. What personal experiences of death do you bring to reading this book?

2. What emotions went through you as you read the opening story of the death and funeral preparations for the two young boys and their aunt and uncle? What might these emotions reveal about your own attitudes toward death?

3. Would you say that you consider death and dying as something negative, positive, or somewhere in between? What is your initial reaction to the suggestion that there is beauty and goodness in death (p. 5)?

4. Have you ever seen someone die? If so, how has that experience shaped how you view death?

5. Caleb Wilde uses the term "death doula" to describe those who lead the dying through their final life stage (p. 7). Think about this role in comparison with the role of a birth doula. How is it

similar? What kind of resources (emotional, spiritual, interpersonal, etc.) are needed in both cases?

6. Wilde writes that his Christian upbringing contributed to his negative view of death, because it framed it as a curse, the result of sin, and something to be fought against and transcended (p. 7). How does your own religious upbringing (or lack thereof) shape your view of death? Do you feel like you need a new death narrative, or are you satisfied with the one you have?

CHAPTER 2: PLAYTIME IN THE CASKET ROOM

1. Have you had any experience with funeral homes? What feelings do they evoke for you?

2. Wilde describes a childhood where life and death were not compartmentalized, but existed under one roof, as both sides of his family lived at their respective funeral homes. Was death a normal part of your life growing up? How did your family approach the fact of death?

3. Growing up in funeral homes meant that Wilde was regularly around dead bodies. How do you react to the idea of being around dead bodies? Does the idea scare you, repulse you, or seem unremarkable to you? What experiences, or lack thereof, do you think contribute to your reaction?

CHAPTER 3: BROKEN OPEN

1. "Death and dying are a sacred art of the human condition, where we learn about ourselves, build community, and contemplate

meaning, much like houses of religion" (p. 20). What do you think it means that death and dying are a sacred art? How might thinking about death as a sacred art push against contemporary practices, which turn death into a medical process?

2. Do you relate to the idea that people have feared death because of the fear of hell? Why or why not?

3. How have you confronted death, mortality, and the deeper questions of life? Or have you avoided them? If and when you have confronted "these inevitabilities," have they broken you open, or broken you apart (p. 26)?

4. The author speaks of death and dying as wild, something we can't control as much as we would like to: "For those who are actively dying, this phase can be an experience of losing control of your physical functions, setting the stage for death to come. When it does, it creates a whole different culture for those left behind, where schedules are always in flux, emotions trump mental function, and love trumps control" (p. 26). How does the lack of control over this area of life make you feel?

5. What kind of wild places (literal or figurative) have you encountered in your own life? How might these encounters prepare you for the wilderness of death?

6. Wilde writes that confronting death at a young age was "the single most difficult and the single most beneficial influence" in his life (p. 27). This goes against the idea that children should be shielded from the void of death. How have you seen death presented to children (in your childhood, with your own chil-

dren, or with children you know)? Discuss what you think is helpful or unhelpful in the approaches you've seen or taken on your own.

CHAPTER 4: DEATH SABBATH

1. Wilde describes the Jewish practice of a death Sabbath—the initial burial; the week after with no music, shoes, or sex; and the thirty days following when mourners work their way back into normal life (p. 31). How does this compare with how your culture normally processes death? Why do you think we often allow ourselves so little time to grieve?

2. "No grief is the same" (p. 37), Wilde says. Whether it is for the death of a loved one or some other loss, what are some ways you've grieved in the past? Would you change how you have grieved in the past, knowing what you know now?

3. Have you ever responded to the invitation to pause for death, to sit in its presence, and listen to it (p. 37)? Describe the experience, if you can. How did you feel? What did you hear? How were you changed by it?

CHAPTER 5: SEARCHING FOR THE DIVINE IN THE DARK

1. Wilde's first experience bringing a dead infant back from the hospital calls into question his belief in a good, loving, all-present, and all-powerful God. What experiences in your life have most challenged your view of God? How did you work through the contradictions? In what ways has your image of God changed throughout your life?

2. How have you wrestled with the problem of evil and suffering?

3. Wilde describes one of the popular ways to explain the problem of evil: through a redefinition of God's power. Read the full paragraph beginning with "One of the more popular paths to remake God . . ." (p. 43). Are you satisfied with this explanation? Why or why not?

CHAPTER 6: SACRED DIRT

1. As a result of seeing how capricious, sad, and heart-wrenching this world could be, the author developed a heaven-centered orientation (p. 45). This, in turn, made tasks like the care of dead people and cleaning the morgue seem small and unimportant, too much of this world and not the next. What are the benefits and pitfalls, in your view, of a heaven-centered orientation?

2. "Heaven may be glorious, but so is the earth, and we miss too much when we focus on one to the exclusion of the other" (p. 50). Discuss this statement. Do you agree or disagree, and why? How do you juggle a hope for the future with an appreciation for what is already in front of you?

3. Wilde returned from his mission trip to Africa with a shifted sense of calling. Instead of "waiting and watching for the life to come," he sensed the call to "be present in the here and now" (p. 51). How has your own sense of calling changed as you've experienced more of life (and death)? In what ways do you feel called to be present-oriented instead of future-oriented?

4. *Tikkun olam* means "the healing of the world" and is accomplished through presence in the midst of pain (p. 51). How have

you seen this idea at work, either in your own life or in events you have witnessed? Can you share an instance where you have received the gift of presence in the midst of pain? What did it mean to you? How was it healing?

CHAPTER 7: THE MYTH OF THE DEATH-CARE AMATEUR

1. Wilde describes the Ricci family as thoroughly involved in the death-care process after the passing of their loved one, not at all afraid to touch death. What do you think about dressing a loved one's dead body for visitation? Would you want to do this yourself? Why or why not?

2. What are some ways you have bought into the modern American vision of self-mastery and control over death (p. 61), or some ways you have been jolted out of this illusion?

3. What do you think would change if we did not simply hand death over to the professionals, as Wilde describes? If Americans were more in touch with death, how would we live differently? Die differently?

CHAPTER 8: FRONT DOOR POLICY

1. What are some ways you have seen death hidden and evaded? What are some ways you have seen death recognized and honored? What effects did the different approaches have on you?

2. "Sacredness is defined by love," Wilde writes (p. 73). By this definition, even our aging, disabled, and dead are sacred, because they are loved. How does this vision compare to how we

normally think of aging, disabled, or dead bodies? If we really considered such bodies as sacred, how might we treat them differently?

3. At the nursing home Luther Acres, the dead are processed through the halls to the front door as staff stand by, to honor them. Can you think of any other ways we might honor death? Why is it important to honor someone in death?

4. "It wasn't just Mrs. Taylor that they were acknowledging; in an indirect way, they were acknowledging me. They were acknowledging my work and my profession in a profoundly special way. I didn't feel like I needed to be hidden. I didn't feel invisible" (p. 74). When we see the beauty in death and honor the dead, how does this change how we see those like Wilde, who work in the service of families during their time of loss?

CHAPTER 9: LISTENING TO THE VOICE OF SILENCE

1. What is easier for you to embrace—Holy Saturday, "that sacred day in the Christian calendar when we worship in doubt, uncertainty, and the feeling of abandonment" (p. 80), or Easter Sunday, with its proclamation of resurrection and fulfillment? Why?

2. Can you describe a time when your faith has been "quieted" (p. 80), the phrase Wilde uses as he tried to make sense of Robbie's death? What kinds of ideas or explanations no longer sufficed? How did you deal with the uncertainty?

3. "Perhaps we fear silence more than death" (p. 82). What, for you, is the most unsettling aspect of silence? Take some time, as

a group or individually, to be silent now. What feelings and reactions come up?

4. How might silence be "the first step in pursuing life" (p. 82)? What would it look like to accept silence in your own life?

CHAPTER 10: GRIEF AS WORSHIP

1. Can you describe any experience in your life where death brought people together and made vulnerability normal, as happened at Chad's funeral?

2. Wilde traces the "death as punishment narrative" back to the Garden of Eden, "where death is the inherited punishment for the sin of Adam and Eve; or, in the phrase used by St. Paul, 'the wages of sin is death' " (p. 90). Do you think it is possible to believe in the story of creation and the fall without also buying into the "death as punishment" narrative? How might it be possible to view death as a result of sin, but also acknowledge that death is not all bad?

3. What are some ways in the past or present that you have been "ashamed by your mortality" and felt that you "will never be enough" (p. 91)? What is your response to reading about Wilde's "mortality positivity," the idea that our humanity, mortality, and limits aren't inherently bad or sinful, but are actually good things that push us to be vulnerable and reach out to others for help?

4. Our desire to transcend our mortality, Wilde says, is related to our image of God as "having no need, a God who is immortal, who isn't dependent on others and who can stand alone unhurt and

untouched by relationships" (p. 93). How does this description compare to your image of God? What is your response to Wilde's description of a God who is vulnerable, who "who stands, maybe even kneels, with us in weakness" (p. 94)?

CHAPTER 11: SARA'S MOSAIC

1. "In death, we find the individual creating community; perhaps nowhere more apparent than at a funeral" (p. 103). Have you experienced the kind of community that forms around someone's death? How is this community different from the kinds of communities we experience in other parts of life?

2. Describe a funeral you've attended, if any, that was done well. Describe a funeral that you've attended, if any, that could have been improved. What are some of the most memorable ways you've seen the dead remembered and "resurrected" at a funeral?

3. "In death, we find both the repulsive and the beautiful; perhaps that is nowhere more apparent than in the gruesome, and yet at times beautiful, art of embalming" (p. 103). Have you ever thought of death, and especially embalming, as something beautiful, artful? Why is seeing death in this tension so hard for us?

CHAPTER 12: HEAVEN ON EARTH

1. With the death of Donnie, Wilde confronts the way that death suspends time—Donnie's daughter doesn't want to leave her dead father's side, everyone else is moving slowly or not moving at all. Have you experienced how time moves differently in mo-

ments like this? Do you think you would be capable of entering with a family into their moment of grief, as Wilde does, over and over again?

2. Have you ever been stricken with compassion fatigue? What kind of self-care and spiritual practices have helped you to regain a sense of compassion and feeling?

3. "To be human is not to be closed off, detached, emotionless, and on a strict schedule. Being human means the opposite: connecting, being fluid, feeling, and—at times—weeping" (p. 112). Much about our technology-dependent and hectic lifestyles seems to go against this definition of humanity. How might getting close to death recover our sense of humanity? How can you protect your humanity in your own life?

4. Wilde writes that "heaven is wherever love reigns" (p. 112). How have your own views of heaven developed throughout your life? What conventional understandings of heaven or hell do you question?

CHAPTER 13: SAM MCKINNEY'S MYSTICISM

1. Wilde writes that death can cultivate mystical belonging or cause more fear and division. What circumstances or attitudes do you think lead to one over the other? How can we as a society respond better to death?

2. What feelings did you have when reading Sam McKinney's story, of finally receiving the acceptance of her church community after her death? Are there communities that have excluded you, or that

you have left behind? Thinking about your own death, would you want to make peace with them somehow?

3. Can you share any personal experiences of death being "the mystical unifier that helps us see the delusions of our tribal divisions and stitch us back together" (p. 125)?

CHAPTER 14: ACTIVE REMEMBERING

1. What is your initial reaction to having a "shrine" for the dead, as Jennifer's parents made at her place at the kitchen table (p. 131)? Where do you think that reaction comes from?

2. How do you, and others in your family, relate to your dead loved ones? Are there ways in which you actively remember them? Are there ways you've tried to find closure and detachment?

3. Recall someone (or something) that you have grieved, or are currently grieving. What kind of "stages" did your grief have, if any? How did the grief change as time went on? If grief is an ongoing part of your life, how have you adjusted to this new reality?

4. Wilde, citing other writers, suggests that the idea that our loved ones become part of us is literal, that "our neural pathways can become reflections of who we love so that our brains have neurologically wired bits and pieces of those closest to us into our mind" (p. 135). Can you give an example of how the people you love have become part of you?

5. What do you think of Wilde's assertion that we have a "continuing relationship with the dead" (p. 138), and that the dead remain

a real presence in the lives of those who live on? Would you agree that "the idea of closure is a myth" (p. 136)?

CHAPTER 15: FINDING MY WORDS

1. Based on your own or others' experiences, what are the most helpful ways someone can accompany a person who is grieving? Wilde lists some phrases that are helpful and unhelpful to say to someone who has just lost a loved one (p. 147–48). Would you add any to the list?

2. Writing, for Wilde, became a way to process after facing the silence and mystery of death over and over. How do you process? Who do you process with?

3. In our churches and communities, how might we "create a space that allows for death talk" (p. 154)? Have you found any such spaces already? What do they look like?

CHAPTER 16: YIN AND YANG

1. Wilde confesses some of his fears of becoming a father—his demanding workload, fear of the death of his children, his fragile psychological state due to wrestling with the silence of death. Whether or not you are a parent, what kinds of fears and uncertainties does the prospect of children (or currently having children) raise for you? If you are a parent, how do you deal with the ongoing pressure of nurturing young lives in the face of many threats of death?

2. Can you relate to the experience of disenfranchised grief, "the kind that is overlooked and unrecognized by society" (p. 161),

either from miscarriage, infertility, or another kind of loss? What social pressures kept you from openly mourning? How did you process your grief?

3. "Death opens up the newness of life" (p. 166). How have you seen this truth play out in your own life?

EPILOGUE

1. How have your thoughts and attitudes toward death changed as you have read this book?

2. Of the ten things Wilde shares about the spirituality of death, which left the most impact on you? Why?

3. Are you ready, as the author eventually was, to allow death into your life? What things might be holding you back? Are there any concrete steps you might take to "embrace death"?